50 GREAT MEMORIES IN GEORGIA
FOOTBALL HISTORY

Whitman
Publishing, LLC
PUBLISHING SINCE 1934
www.whitman.com

50 Great Memories In Georgia Football History

www.whitman.com
© 2012 Whitman Publishing, LLC

ISBN: 0794837239
Printed and assembled in the United States of America

Scan the QR code above to browse
Whitman Publishing's full selection
of sports and specialty books.

TABLE OF CONTENTS

HOW DO YOU DEFINE THE GREATEST MEMORIES?

By Loran Smith

The "greatest" memories in most any sport cannot be established conclusively, and any attempt is not without emotion-provoking decisions. Any of the estimated 54,000 fans (excepting the Auburn partisans) who saw Georgia's Fran Tarkenton throw a 13-yard touchdown pass to Bill Herron to defeat Auburn 14-13 in 1959 in Sanford Stadium would have difficulty voting for any other game being greater than that one.

Georgia had been down but came back with a Cinderella season under coach Wallace Butts, who won his fourth and final Southeastern Conference title. Tarkenton was the greatest hero in the state for months after the game, just like Frank Sinkwich and Charley Trippi were following the Rose Bowl, Jan. 1, 1943 — although Sinkwich and Trippi did not hang around to celebrate and to be toasted, because they immediately went off to war. Adulation for them, however, never retreated.

Except for a surviving player, it would be difficult to find a living Bulldog who saw the Rose Bowl game, as very few fans and alumni made it to Pasadena. Those of us who came along decades later can't appreciate that game unless it is through scrapbooks and faded newspaper clippings. There are no video replays or flashbacks for the most part, although there is a Rose Bowl film (remember, the game did take place near Hollywood). But anyone starting out a career in sports journalism today, even with little information and no eyewitnesses, would know the importance of winning the Rose Bowl.

How about those who saw Lamar "Racehorse" Davis' touchdown catch with no time left on the clock to defeat Auburn in Columbus in 1941? Or how about those who were humbled by Theron Sapp's 1-yard plunge that broke the drought versus Tech in 1957? The ecstasy of being in the moment, the thrill of being there, would give any memory the highest value when ranking highlights of Georgia football.

Those who assembled in Sanford Stadium for the 1965 "flea-flicker" upset of Alabama may consider — based on the drama and the fact Alabama was defending national champion under coach Paul "Bear" Bryant — that as Georgia's greatest moment. Likewise, those on hand in the Superdome, Jan. 1, 1981, who saw Scott Woerner make the interception that gave Georgia the last possession against Notre Dame and clinch victory in the National Championship Game surely would vote that as Georgia's greatest moment.

When picking great moments, you have to factor in the competition and the era. Tarkenton, for example, who went on to become the most prolific passer in the NFL at one point, completed only 186 of 503 passes in his Georgia career — certainly not a harbinger of what would follow in the NFL. The one-platoon rules of his day keep one from ranking Tarkenton as one of the all-time collegiate quarterbacks. Because of the rules, he simply doesn't have the numbers. He is, however, a fabled hero for that one pass in 1959 that brought about a championship.

Settling on the 50 greatest memories in Georgia football history required an informal criteria based on what the game meant to the Bulldog program, how — and if — it influenced a championship, and whether it brought about a memorable, lasting and unforgettable moment.

Have you ever noticed that the team winning a championship gets more all-star selections and honors? Win a national championship and your coach becomes coach of the year, and your quarterback or your running back becomes a favorite for the Heisman Trophy.

It is obvious that, following the early days, the three greatest eras at Georgia were those influenced by the championship runs of Wallace Butts, Vince Dooley and Mark Richt. It is from those eras that most of the greatest memories come.

However, I don't see how any of us could not vote for the performance of end Vernon "Catfish" Smith in the 1929 game with Yale as being one of the most unforgettable moments in Georgia history. Except for Dan Magill — Georgia's indefatigable and multifaceted hero — and perhaps a couple of others, few living people saw that game. Think about the circumstances and the setting: Georgia is dedicating a sparkling new stadium, the biggest and best in the Southland; Yale, the scourge of the East, has come to town for a sensational matchup. For many Southerners, it essentially was the replaying of the Civil War. All Catfish did was score every point in a monumental 15-0 upset!

Tailgating had to have been at an all-time high for the Yale game. Old-timers for years afterward said that a record number of Cokes were sold that day. Although there is nothing official to substantiate it, I have been told by some who were around for the game that a record amount of moonshine was also consumed. The times, of course, would dictate that circumstance.

Singling out *the* play in a big game in a championship season is never easy. Take the Georgia-Tennessee game in 1980, for example. There were multiple heroes that night. Joe Happe, playing with a broken hand, forced a fumbled punt late in the third quarter, which led to the first Bulldog points, a safety. Tennessee could have won the game with a drive in the fourth quarter, with Georgia leading 17-16, but

Nate Taylor forced a fumble and Pat McShea recovered. Tennessee, on Georgia's next possession, played tenacious defense with the objective of bringing about a game-winning field-goal opportunity, keeping Georgia backed up to its own goal line. Then Jim Broadway, who became the punter when the regular punter, Mark Malkiewicz, was injured preseason, delivered a career punt of 47 yards to midfield. The Georgia defense closed the deal. Herschel Walker, with two bull rushes for touchdowns, rightly became the game's hero, but Georgia doesn't win without Happe, Taylor, McShea, Broadway and others who contributed to a victory in an undefeated national championship season.

Under Mark Richt, there have been four trips to the SEC Championship Game, and twice the Bulldogs won the SEC title. There have been many thrilling moments during Richt's time, highlighted by the 45-16 thrashing of LSU between the hedges in 2004 and the D.J. Shockley-led upset of the Tigers in the 2005 SEC Championship Game. And, in his first season, who could forget the 26-24 hobnail boot game in Knoxville?

To get to the Georgia Dome in 2002 required an unforgettable moment at Auburn, when David Greene threw a fourth-down 15-yard perfect strike to Michael Johnson. Greene put it where only a leaping Johnson could get to the ball. The catch gave Georgia the SEC East title.

The defensive genius of David Pollack when he stole the ball against South Carolina in 2002 and against Wisconsin in the 2004 Outback Bowl are as memorable as any defensive plays in Georgia history. Then there was the comeback against Purdue in the 1999 Outback Bowl, when, down 25-0, the Bulldogs rallied to win 28-25.

How many great memories are missing? Like beauty being in the eye of the beholder, there are probably many, but we hope you enjoy recalling the selection herein. It's not definitive, but we think it is more than representative.

How It All Began

Jan. 30, 1892 · Georgia 50, Mercer 0

Football in winter? That is when it all began at the University of Georgia, Jan. 30, 1892, with the Bulldogs hosting Mercer on a grassless field barely a hundred yards south of Lumpkin Street in Athens.

John Stegeman, Bulldog historian, wrote that a thousand townspeople and students gathered to watch the first intercollegiate game in the Deep South. The game was played by rules outlined by UGA's first coach, Dr. Charles Herty, who had picked up a rules book when he was at Johns Hopkins University, where he had enrolled to study chemistry. Johns Hopkins is where Herty was introduced to the game of "foot-ball."

Football offered an outlet to release energy, but the main thing was that it created an environment for competition. Because it appeared to be little more than organized roughhousing, the game drew instant appeal. While no one ever conducted an in-depth interview with Herty, he apparently was fascinated by the Americanized game of rugby, but he had to have believed that those who succeeded in life were those who could best the competition. Football was an avenue for young men to become exposed to the reality of the vicissitudes of life.

A review of old photographs and Stegeman's book, *Touchdown* (written with Skeets Willingham), reveals that Georgia's initial game of football was played with only 11 men. Turtleneck-style sweaters were worn, along with padded pants and knee-length stockings. Shoes were nondescript, although in 1892 Goodyear — taking advantage of vulcanization (the melting of rubber and fabric together) — came out with a lightweight shoe with flexibility, which led to the creation of "Keds." For Georgia's first football team, it pretty much was a case of the players fashioning their own uniforms.

They used the old bladder-type ball, rounded and compatible with drop-kicking extra points. A touchdown counted four points and a conversion kick was worth two points. Georgia scored on its first posses-

(Preceding page) The first football team the University of Georgia fielded in 1892 consisted of, front row, left to right: Julian R. Lane, Frank J. Herty, W.N. Gramling, Henry C. Brown, John C. Kimball and L.D. Fricks. Back row: A.O. Halsey, E.P. Howell Jr., E.W. Frey, George Shackelford and Rufus B. Nalley. (Above) Nalley, the left tackle on offense, was one of the larger players on the squad at 6-foot, 165 pounds. He was outweighed only by Frey at 202 pounds and Shackelford at 175 pounds. Herty was the cousin of Dr. Charles Herty, better known as "The Father of Georgia Football."

sion, and a pet goat adorned with red and black ribbons served as the mascot.

Georgia had tried to get Mercer to organize a team for a game in the fall of 1891, but that didn't happen, which is why the first game was played in January. The score, 50-0, might have been an indication of "insufficient interest" in the game on the Mercer campus in Macon. Tackle A.O. Halsey told historian Stegeman that Georgia actually scored 60 points against Mercer. Late in the game, he explained, the scorekeeper "walked across Broad Street to buy a bottle of booze." He missed two touchdowns and a conversion, Halsey claimed.

This is why I have always maintained that Georgia's first football game was also its first football tailgate party!

A RIVALRY IS BORN

Feb. 20, 1892
Auburn 10, Georgia 0

(Left) An artist's rendition of an early Georgia football uniform. (Opposite page) Dr. Charles Herty was the school's first football coach, and became a famous chemist as well.

The story of the first game between Georgia and Auburn was also one of two old friends, who met at Johns Hopkins and became pioneer academicians for their respective campuses — George Petrie at Auburn and Charles Herty at Georgia.

They met while studying for PhDs and learned about the new American game, "foot-ball." It was only natural that they, the founding coaches at their respective institutions, would "get up a game" between Georgia and Auburn at Piedmont Park in Atlanta on Feb. 20, 1892. Auburn won 10-0, and the Deep South's oldest football rivalry began.

History tells us more about these two professors than about the game. Petrie was the first Alabamian to earn a PhD. At Auburn, he founded the history department and the graduate school. Like Herty at Georgia, he became the school's first football coach.

Herty, a chemist, would earn everlasting fame and appreciation for revolutionizing the turpentine industry in the United States, developing the process in which pine pulp could be turned into newsprint.

It is curiously noteworthy that the players in the days of Petrie and Herty were legitimate student-athletes. It was unquestionably an amateur exercise. A degree was paramount for those who played the game, a contrast to the game today in all too many instances. Interestingly, Herty (1-1) and Petrie (2-2) each retired after one year of coaching, and, even more interesting, they worked for free.

There is no question that Charles Herty was a great Georgian. To grasp the magnitude of his contributions to the state, simply slide your fingers across the pages of this book. In addition to creating the pulp-to-paper process, Herty originated football in Athens. What could be more important to the state of Georgia today than the pine tree industry and Georgia football?

As for that first game between Georgia and Auburn, historian John Stegeman's account from his research and with conversations with players on the Bulldogs' first team reveals that an estimated 2,000 people showed up for the game, making their way to Piedmont Park by "horsecar, electric car, dray, dos-a-dos, T-cart, and tally ho." Stegeman noted that Georgia Tech students were in the stands early and were neutral, as they pulled for neither team. "Instead, they sang risqué ditties of their own and laughed as the ladies blushed."

There is no box score and no statistical sheet to document the details of the game. There are few headlines and no game-action photos, but it is one of the most important games in history of the two institutions. It established the Deep South's oldest football rivalry.

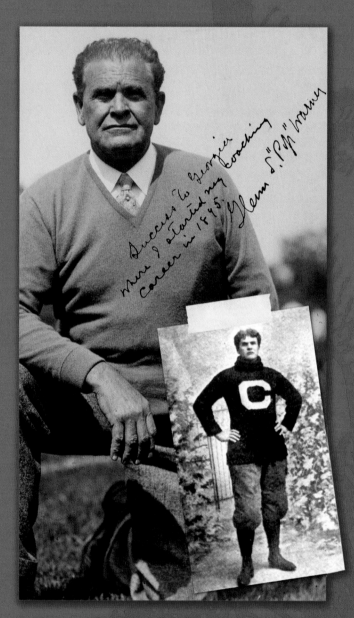

Pop Warner Comes To Georgia

1895 & 1896

(Lower left) When Glenn "Pop" Warner arrived at Georgia to become head coach in 1895, he was wearing a Cornell letter sweater with a "C" on the front. (Far left) Many years later, Warner autographed this photo and donated it to UGA. Warner became one of the greatest coaches in college football history, and is enshrined in the College Football Hall of Fame.

Glenn "Pop" Warner is perhaps best known for coaching the great Jim Thorpe at the Carlisle Indian Industrial School in Carlisle, Pennsylvania. Before that, Warner coached the University of Georgia football team in 1895 and 1896.

Warner had come to Georgia to coach a year after he had captained the Cornell gridiron team and earned a law degree. Photos of him during his time in Athens are of him in his Cornell letter sweater with a big "C" on the front.

It was reported that when Warner saw the grassless, rock-strewn field on north campus where the football team played its games, he was in shock. Then, when only a dozen players showed up for practice, he was ready to return home.

When Georgia played St. Mary's in San Francisco in 1950, Dan Magill, Bulldog publicist, looked up the aging Warner and reminisced with him about the old coach's time in Athens. Warner spoke favorably of his days in Athens.

A pictorial display in the Butts-Mehre Building on campus reflects Warner's Hall of Fame career. There is a photo of Warner that bears an inscription to the University of Georgia, "Success to Georgia where I started my coaching career in 1895. Glenn 'Pop' Warner."

In his brief time in Athens, Warner displayed clever coaching ability. His 1896 team was Georgia's first undefeated team with a 4-0 record. In John Stegeman's *Touchdown*, there is a reference that Warner remembered student affection for a new drink called "Coca-Cola." One can only imagine what might have happened had the Georgia coach had the good sense to purchase Coca-Cola stock, but, as Stegeman pointed out, there wasn't much opportu-

nity for such investment on his salary of $34 a week.

Warner's 1895 team posted a 3-4 record, but the coach returned in 1896 with a raise of $6 per week. Georgia went undefeated in four games, giving up only 22 points against Wofford (26-0), North Carolina (24-16), Sewanee (26-0) and Auburn (12-6).

It would be Warner's last season in Athens. He would move on to coaching assignments — in addition to Carlisle — at Iowa State, Cornell, Pittsburgh and Stanford.

(Above) Georgia's 1896 team went undefeated under Warner, winning all four games they played, while giving up only 22 total points.

Warner coached in the 1895 game against North Carolina, in which a fierce Georgia rush caused the North Carolina punter to wildly fling the snap in frustration. The ball came down into the arms of a startled teammate, who raced for a touchdown, causing some to say this was the first forward pass in college football. Warner protested long and loudly, but the referee allowed the score to stand because he "didn't see it."

A Mother's Strength Prevailed

Oct. 30, 1897
Virginia 17, Georgia 4

(Left) Georgia's Richard Vonalbade Gammon died from a head injury suffered against Virginia in October 1897. The public wanted football banned in Georgia because of his death and several others, but Rosalind Burns Gammon, Richard's mother, wrote a letter to the governor urging him not to sign the bill into law that the legislature had passed. Gov. William Y. Atkinson then vetoed the bill. (Opposite page) This bronze plaque honoring Mrs. Gammon and her son is on display in the Butts-Mehre Building on the UGA campus.

The evolution of football was not without incident or controversy. It is a physical game and has been since its inception, having evolved from a rugby scrum. Wrestling was a common activity in the lives of young people, dating back to the original Olympic Games. It was a fulfilling and spontaneous exercise, permeating campus life in the early days of higher education.

Initially, as everybody knows, football was played without helmets. The coming of the forward pass was, in part, the result of football players dying from playing the sport. Passing forced teams to change alignments so that they were not tightly bunched together.

There was an outcry against football in the late 1800s because of the plethora of fatalities from football competition. It reached a crescendo in late October 1897, when Georgia's Richard Vonalbade Gammon died from head injuries suffered in a game with Virginia in Atlanta.

Von Gammon, as he was known, had played for Glenn "Pop" Warner and was a passionate advocate of the game of football. He grew up in an athletic family in Rome, Georgia. "The Gammons were always playing games and involved in outdoor activity and competition," Lila Patton, a descendant of the family, once told me in an afternoon conversation one spring that took place near the Etowah River, which flows through Rome.

Affection for sport apparently contributed to the attitude of Von Gammon's mother, Rosalind Burns Gammon, who during her period of grieving wrote a letter that influenced a stirring and far-reaching decision by Gov. William Y. Atkinson.

In the Virginia game Oct. 30, 1897, Von Gammon apparently flung himself into a pileup on a play from scrimmage and came crashing down head first on his chin, hitting the hardpan earth with great force. The resulting concussion and brain injury brought about his death the next day.

With the legislature in session, public opinion segued in the direction of banning the sport in Georgia. The legislature quickly agreed and passed a bill outlawing football. All that was needed to ban the game in its infancy in Georgia was the stroke of the governor's pen.

When Von Gammon's mother heard the news, she immediately wrote Gov. Atkinson, pleading him not to sign the bill into law. Although she was saddened by the tragic death of her son, her impassioned plea asked the governor not to take away a game that he and his friends loved so much. The letter deeply touched the state's chief executive, as he refused to sign the bill.

If you visit the Butts-Mehre Building on campus, there is a beautiful plaque depicting a mother holding her fallen son — in memory of Von Gammon. It was given to the University of Georgia by the Virginia players who were distraught when they heard the news of Von Gammon's death. The inscription reads: "A Mother's Strength Prevailed."

McWhorter Surprises Georgia Tech

Nov. 19, 1910 · Georgia 11, Georgia Tech 6

The final score of the final game of the season in 1910 brought about perpetual rejoicing in Athens: Georgia 11, Georgia Tech 6. For the first time in seven years, the Red and Black waved proudly over the state.

There was no game between the schools in 1908, but Tech had won five in a row previously. This was the John Heisman era at Tech, but in 1910, the Bob McWhorter era began at Georgia. The upper hand in the series belonged to the Red and Black. McWhorter would lead his team to victory over the archrival four years in a row.

McWhorter, who played for Alex Cunningham, lived a storybook life. He was a native son who led the Bulldogs to memorable heights — most notably against Alabama and Georgia Tech. All-Southern four straight years. Georgia's first All-American. First Georgia player elected to the College Football Hall of Fame. Career as professor of law at his alma mater. And mayor of Athens.

Cunningham, the cagey coach, and McWhorter, the versatile back, would arrive in Athens together. McWhorter had prepped at Gordon Institute, where he learned the finer points of the game under Cunningham, who was ingenious with the development of trick plays.

"McWhorter," wrote John Stegeman in *Touchdown*, "was perfectly willing to participate in the prep-school tricks that his coach installed in the Georgia attack, as they were part of the fun. To make a grueling touchdown was one thing, but to score out of nowhere without being touched brought quite another kind of satisfaction. Take Georgia's first scrimmage play in 1911 on the

new athletic field in the Lumpkin Street valley. McWhorter (in a numberless jersey) hid out on the sideline as a 'sleeper,' his coach's favorite play, and took a long touchdown pass forty yards distant from the nearest defender."

One of McWhorter's partners in crime when it came to tricking the opposition was George "Kid" Woodruff, who would later coach the Bulldogs for a dollar a year. A particularly noteworthy trick play in McWhorter's career came at Sewanee when Georgia tried one of its favorite ploys — the headgear trick.

"Against Tennessee," Stegeman wrote, "Walter Lucas, a guard whose helmet was painted the color of the ball, suddenly passed it back, center-like, to McWhorter, who along with a detail of blockers, swept to his right. Woodruff, meanwhile, sneaking

(Preceding page) Bob McWhorter was Georgia's first All-American, and the first Georgia player elected to the College Football Hall of Fame. In 1910, he helped Georgia beat Georgia Tech for the first time in seven years. (Above) The Georgia Bulldogs of 1910.

the real ball from center, tore off in the opposite direction for a long gain."

The modest McWhorter, one of Georgia's most accomplished players ever, is said to have never mentioned his signature honors in public.

The Water-Bucket Play

Oct. 26, 1912
Georgia 13, Alabama 9

Coach Alex Cunningham, a military man, functioned in football like a counter-intelligence officer. His personality was akin to the serious practical joker who gains great satisfaction from con games that deliver a coup de gras. Only the victim takes exception.

Perhaps Coach Alex's boldest and most audacious effort came in the 1912 Alabama game in Columbus. With his penchant for trick plays, he caused the opposition to stay on constant alert for "Cunningham's craftiness" and shenanigans that were a standard part of the Georgia repertoire. This time, he employed the blatant use of camouflage.

He dressed his quarterback, Alonzo Awtrey, in street clothes and had him carry a water bucket on the sideline. Not even the most curious of surveillance would have suspected that Georgia was "up to something."

Tempers would soon be flaring, as Awtrey, on the first play from scrimmage, dropped his water bucket, raced onto the field and moved past the Alabama defenders for a long pass reception. One Bama defender was able to catch up with Awtrey before he crossed the goal line.

A donnybrook immediately ensued, and, according to John Stegeman, caused suspension of play for over half an hour. Representing Georgia on the sideline was professor John Morris, who soon was approached by a professor from Alabama who demanded of Morris that he ask Cunningham, in the name of sportsmanship, to recall the play. Morris, according to Stegeman, refused — whereupon Morris was flattened by the Alabama athletic director.

Eventually, play was resumed, but Bob McWhorter, Georgia's great back, fumbled to Alabama. After that, players of both teams settled down and played football as it was meant to be played — blocking, tackling and no circumvention of the rules. The final score was Georgia 13, Alabama 9, in a classic and thrilling college football game.

(Preceding page) Coach Alex Cunningham had a penchant for calling trick plays. One of the classics came against Alabama in 1912 involving his quarterback wearing street clothes and carrying a water bucket. (Above) Walter Lucas was a guard on the 1912 team.

Beating Alabama was a big coup. Cunningham was the toast of Athens for his success on the gridiron, but nothing gave the community more of a lift than his four straight victories over Georgia Tech and John Heisman.

A *Pandora* cartoonist, following Georgia's 14-0 defeat of Tech in 1913, created a cartoon. In the caption, you can see that the word "Dawg" first appeared in print long before the era of Vince Dooley and Herschel Walker.

It would not be long before Cunningham would return to the military as World War I caused the cancellation of all games in 1917-18. He was welcomed back to the military, where "real" espionage would take priority in his life.

NEWLY MINTED
BULLDOGS BLOCK BAMA

Nov. 20, 1920 · Georgia 21, Alabama 14

(Left) Sanford Field served double duty as UGA's football field and baseball stadium. (Opposite page) Buck Cheves, sixth from the left in the front row, picked up a blocked drop-kick attempt and ran 87 yards for the winning touchdown against Alabama in 1920.

Football at Georgia was important historically, but the Roaring Twenties brought about a new objective for alumni and friends — win a championship. Eventually, the hue and cry would be for Georgia to play in a bowl, namely the Rose Bowl, but the Southern Intercollegiate Athletic Association championship remained emotionally significant for everyone.

What is most relevant about the 1920 season (8-0-1 record) is that a fiercely fought tie versus Virginia in Charlottesville led to Georgia becoming known as the Bulldogs. Cliff Wheatley, an Atlanta sportswriter, referred to the team's "bulldog tenacity" after Georgia stopped Virginia on five sets of downs within the 10-yard line. This led to a hard-fought 0-0 tie.

To win the SIAA championship, however, it took a sensational defensive play for Georgia to defeat Alabama 21-14 at Ponce de Leon Park in Atlanta to claim the Southern title.

Alabama was highly touted for its offense that season, while Georgia had played seven games without giving up a touchdown. Only Oglethorpe, with a field goal, had scored on Georgia, now officially known as the Bulldogs. There was much advance publicity about the game, pitting the explosive Alabama offense against the impregnable Georgia defense. In the end, it was Georgia's defense that turned out to be the difference.

Within the first five minutes, Georgia had scored two touchdowns. End Paige Bennett scooped up a fumble and raced across the goal line for the first, while guard Hugh "Puss" Whelchel — who blocked 19 kicks in his career in Athens — blocked an Alabama punt and tackle Artie Pew grabbed the bounding ball and scored to put Georgia up 14-0.

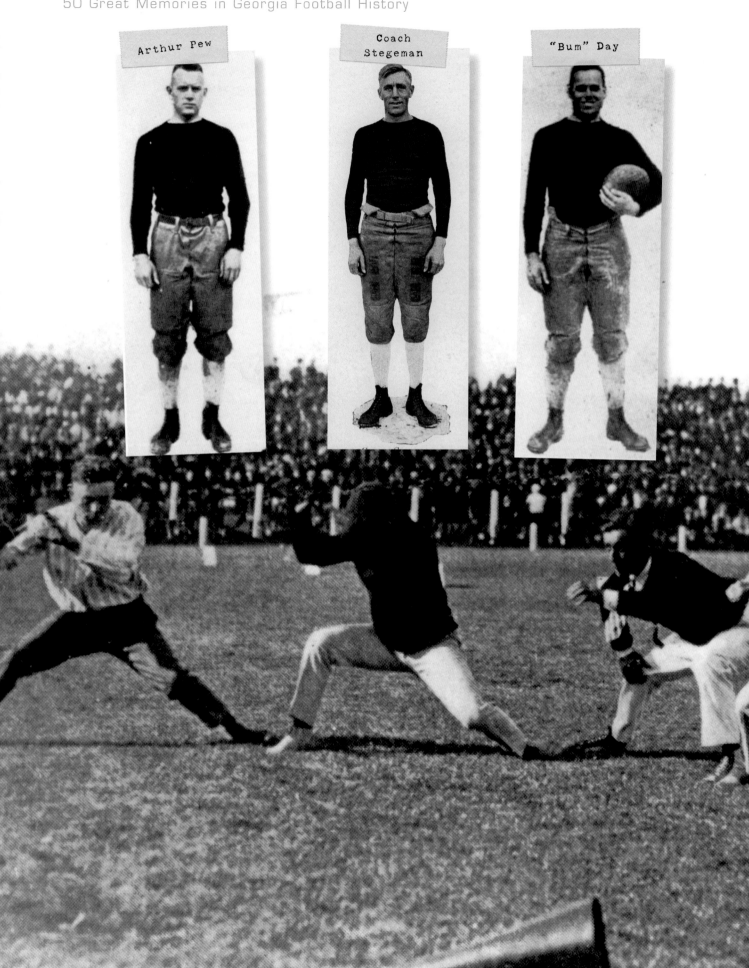

Arthur Pew

Coach Stegeman

"Bum" Day

Puss Whelchel

Alabama's vaunted offense then gained control of the game, scoring two touchdowns to bring about a 14-14 tie. The initial Bama score was the first time that season that Georgia had given up a touchdown. By the time the fourth quarter rolled around, it appeared that further scoring was not likely. However, late in the game, Georgia fumbled the ball at its 20-yard line. Alabama could only make 3 yards in three plays and called on Talty O'Conner for a field-goal attempt to win the game and break Georgia hearts.

However, Whelchel again rose to the occasion, making perhaps the biggest play of his career. He blocked the drop-kick attempt, and Buck Cheves picked up the ball and dashed 87 yards for the winning touchdown.

Sixty-two years later, when John Stegeman interviewed Cheves, his memory was clear and concise. "I lined up on Puss Whelchel's rump and told him, 'If you block it, I'll run it back for a touchdown.'"

He did and Buck did, and Georgia had its first football championship.

(Preceding page, top, left to right) Arthur Pew scooped up a blocked punt and scored to give Georgia a 14-0 lead over Alabama. Coach John Stegeman's 1920 squad finished with an 8-0-1 record. A.M. "Bum" Day served as captain on the 1920 team. (Preceding page, bottom) Cheerleading in the early years was an all-male activity. (Above) Hugh "Puss" Whelchel came up with two crucial blocked kicks that resulted in touchdowns in the 1920 Alabama game. Whelchel blocked a total of 19 kicks in his career at Georgia.

VIDEO FROM 1929

SCAN TO WATCH

YALE GAME

CATFISH STARS IN SANFORD DEDICATION

Oct. 12, 1929 · Georgia 15, Yale 0

(Right) Vernon "Catfish" Smith scored all of Georgia's 15 points against Yale in 1929. (Opposite page) Newly constructed Sanford Stadium was built next to old Sanford Field.

1929
ENTER GATE
2
YALE
VS
GEORGIA
SATURDAY
OCTOBER 12,
2 P.M.
EASTERN TIME

DEDICATION
SANFORD STADIUM FIELD
UNIVERSITY OF GEORGIA
YALE
VERSUS
GEORGIA
SATURDAY, OCTOBER 12, 1929
KICK-OFF 2 P.M. EASTERN TIME
PRICE $3.00
SCORE YALE GEORGIA — HOLD YOUR OWN TICKET

NORTH SIDE
AISLE 7
ROW 32
SEAT 16

Georgia dedicated its sparkling new stadium, named for Steadman V. Sanford, on Oct. 12, 1929. The game was a classic. Bulldog end Vernon "Catfish" Smith scored all 15 points against Yale, the scourge of The East, which never mounted a serious scoring threat. A book could have been written about events and circumstances surrounding the game.

First of all, the 30,000-seat stadium, the classiest in the Southland, was brought to existence to eliminate the home-field advantage that Georgia Tech had enjoyed for years. Following Georgia's 33-0 defeat of their cross-state rival in Athens in 1899, the game was annually held in Atlanta to attract a larger gate.

From that point until 1924, Tech hosted the game annually and held the advantage with a 10-6-2 record. The rivalry was halted from 1919 through 1924, owing to a big feud. Then in 1925-26, each team won at Grant Field, but Bulldog fans were incensed following the 1927 game when Georgia could have earned a Rose Bowl invitation but the Yellow Jackets upset the "Dream and Wonder" team 12-0. Legend has it that it rained that week but that Georgia Tech also watered down the field to great excess. With the soggy conditions, Georgia's smallish but swift backs could not gain ground. Nonetheless, the Bulldogs were named national champions in two polls recognized by the NCAA.

Even with the national title, Dr. Sanford was so outraged by Tech's victory that he would see that Georgia developed the finest stadium in the South. Sanford succeeded by inviting alumni and friends to contribute by signing personal bank notes for the building of a new stadium over Tanyard Creek in the hollow at the bottom of Lumpkin Street. The stadium cost roughly $300,000, but contributions flowed in and the athletic association only had to borrow $180,000 — an unbelievable bargain, even for those times. To secure the loan, "guarantors" signed notes, most for $1,000. Black Tuesday, the day of the stock market crash, came 17 days later on Oct. 29, 1929. None of the notes were ever called — a highlight in UGA history.

Many more than 30,000 fans, not counting those perched on nearby buildings and hanging from the trees, found their way into the stadium for the dedication game, which was played in bright sunshine with the infant hedges, a little more than two feet high, encircling the field.

Catfish Smith, a native of Macon and also a star in basketball and baseball, was elected to the College Football Hall of Fame in 1979. His performance against Yale — along with his colorful personality, no doubt — had an effect on his selection.

One headline in a New York paper applauded Smith's big day: "Catfish 15, Yale 0."

(Preceding page) Catfish Smith recovers a punt blocked by Bobby Rose to give Georgia an early lead against Yale. (Above left) Joe Boland served as captain for the 1929 Bulldogs. (Above right) Steadman V. Sanford started out as an English professor at Georgia in 1903, then became president in 1932 and chancellor in 1935.

GEORGIA STUNS SEVEN BLOCKS OF GRANITE

Nov. 21, 1936 · Georgia 7, Fordham 7

Third-ranked Fordham was heavily favored against the 4-4 Bulldogs heading into the game at Yankee Stadium. In addition to Pete Tinsley, end Asa Candler also had a big game against the Rams and the "Seven Blocks of Granite."

Elijah Page "Pete" Tinsley gave Fordham's offensive line a lesson on quickness, agility and relentless determination.

Before the rules changed with respect to ties, it was obvious that nobody lost the game. However, if you were the heavy favorite to win and an underdog team left the field without losing, it made the underdog feel like it was the victor and left the favorite feeling like it had lost.

That was the case Nov. 21, 1936, in New York.

Fordham, like several other colleges in metropolitan New York — Columbia, NYU and Manhattan, for example — were competitive in football at the time. The National Football League had not become established to compete for fans. College football was big in New York, and Fordham, in its heyday, played before sold-out crowds at the Polo Grounds. In 1936, the Rams had what many thought was the greatest offensive line and defensive line in history of college

PETE TINSLEY

GUARD 1938-1945

UNIVERSITY OF GEORGIA

This plaque honoring Tinsley is on display
in the Green Bay Packer Hall of Fame.

(Above) Forrest "Spec" Towns, an end on the 1936 Bulldogs, won a gold medal in the 110-meter high hurdles at the 1936 Olympics in Berlin. UGA coach Harry Mehre then sent Towns a telegram reading, "Minor sports are over, come home." (Below) Julius Caesar Hall served as co-captain on the 1936 team.

football. The line, featuring consensus All-Americans Ed Franco and Alex Wojciechowicz, was known as the "Seven Blocks of Granite." Vince Lombardi, who would go on to iconic fame as head coach of the Green Bay Packers, was a member of the famed line.

The Rams, who were heavily favored and who had a Rose Bowl invitation on their collective minds, were victimized by the play of Georgia's Pete Tinsley, one of the toughest and most combative players in history of Georgia football.

Before the game, coach Harry Mehre, a native of Huntington, Indiana, rendered an impassioned message to the native Southerners that this was a time to avenge the defeat of the South in the Civil War. Elijah Page "Pete" Tinsley gave the Rams and the Seven Blocks of Granite a lesson on the football values of quickness, agility and relentless determination. He appeared in his opponent's backfield so frequently that the Rams thought he might have lined up back there.

Tinsley was a born-again Rebel. Once, at the downtown Varsity restaurant, a couple of players with Northern addresses brought up the Civil War, and Pete took offense, suggesting that "with a little more ammunition and a few sacks of parched corn" the outcome would have been different. "You boys ain't so tough," Tinsley threatened them. With that, he pulled out a razor blade from his pocket and slit the soft side of his jaw, poked his cigar through the slit, and puffed away. "Those Yankee boys' knees buckled to the ground," Pete said with a laugh as he told me the story in his adopted hometown of Florence, Wisconsin, late in his life.

Tinsley was elected to the Green Bay Packer Hall of Fame as a tackle in 1979. Living only 116 miles from Green Bay, he often visited the adoring hometown of the Packers. When he was introduced to Vince Lombardi, he thought it would be interesting to ask the Packer czar about the tie with Fordham. Lombardi thought otherwise.

"He grunted and refused to talk about it," Tinsley said with a laugh. "He glared at me and then walked away."

WALLY BUTTS BECOMES HEAD COACH

1939

(Left) Wallace Butts took over the Georgia football program in 1939. When he retired from coaching in 1960, his record was 140-86-9. (Below) Frank Sinkwich on the run against Georgia Tech in 1939. (Opposite page) Vassa Cate battles for a big gain against Auburn in 1939.

When Harry Mehre's time at Georgia came to a conclusion, Bill Hartman Jr. and a couple of his teammates lobbied with university officials to hire their former Georgia Military College coach, Wallace Butts. At the time, Butts had developed a sensational prep-school coaching reputation and had moved on to Male High School in Louisville, Kentucky, where he was enjoying championship success.

Hartman was captain of Mehre's last team, but when his Bulldog coach moved on, he wanted to see his prep coach enjoy an opportunity to coach on the college level.

The university did not hire Butts, but when Joel Hunt — a big star at Texas A&M as a player — became Bulldog coach, he hired Butts to coach the ends. Hunt only lasted a year. When Hunt was forced out, James Wallace Butts became the Bulldogs' 20th head coach.

Butts was eminently qualified to coach on the college level. His insightful and ingenious knowledge of the passing game brought him the reputation of being one of the most knowledgeable football strategists in the sport. If he were coaching today, he would enjoy guru status, and young coaches would be flocking to his door to talk about the nuances of the passing game.

Butts' other asset was recruiting. Having coached at Madison A&M, Butts was familiar with high school coaches in other parts of the county, especially Pennsylvania and Ohio. The old A&M schools offered work scholarships — where players got free room, board and tuition — a program that attracted a lot of players regionally. They worked in the fields, went to class and practiced football, thereby being afforded the opportunity to further their education and also compete athletically.

In addition, Butts had contacts with Georgia alumni and friends across the county. They would call and advise him on prospects in the areas where they were working or had settled permanently. One example was Harold Ketran, the Coca-Cola bottler in Wilkes-Barre, Pennsylvania. It was Ketran who sent Charley Trippi to Georgia.

In 1939, Butts recruited one of the best freshman classes in history of the University of Georgia. Led by Frank Sinkwich, who would win the Heisman Trophy in 1942, UGA smashed all competition, scoring 166 points in three games and becoming known as the "Point-a-Minute Bullpups." Trippi enrolled the next year, and the Bulldogs became a powerhouse.

Butts, to the delight of the Athens community, got Georgia in the bowl business with an Orange Bowl bid his third season. The Rose Bowl followed, and one can only imagine what he would have been able to accomplish had World War II not interrupted football in Athens. When he retired from coaching in 1960, his career record was 140-86-9.

A Bell-Ringer to Go Bowling

Nov. 29, 1941 · Georgia 21, Georgia Tech 0

(Left) The 1941 game between Georgia and Georgia Tech was a hard-fought battle. (Opposite page) Frank Sinkwich, pictured here in the 1941 Alabama game, helped the Bulldogs earn an invitation to the Orange Bowl with the 21-0 victory over Georgia Tech.

In 1927 when Georgia missed out on a Rose Bowl invitation, it would be 14 years before the local gentry in Athens got its hopes up again for a bowl opportunity.

Frank Sinkwich was a junior in 1941, and the "Point-a-Minute Bullpups" had come of age. As sophomores, the highlight of the "experience gaining" campaign was a 21-19 victory over Georgia Tech, but there wasn't much else to boast about, as their record was an undistinguished 5-4-1. The seasoning, however, would take effect a year later, as Hitler's armies began gaining momentum in Europe.

The Bulldogs won nine games in 1941, losing 27-14 to Alabama in Birmingham and finishing in a 14-14 tie against the Harry Mehre-coached Ole Miss Rebels.

The season, in retrospect, was of lasting import in that the Bulldogs were gaining traction under Butts. The populace could sense it, too. Everybody wanted the Bulldogs to win enough games to warrant a bowl invitation. A bowl invitation was confirmation that you had an elite program.

But to get there, the Bulldogs had to win their last game against Georgia Tech in Atlanta. The Dogs had disposed of Florida, Centre and Dartmouth, giving up only nine points in three games — after the sensational last-minute win over Auburn on Nov. 1 in Columbus. That unforgettable game was when Sinkwich threw a 40-yard touchdown pass to Lamar "Racehorse" Davis with no time left on the clock.

That brought the Bulldogs regional and national attention, but there was still one game left, which would determine the Orange Bowl's decision. The Bulldogs came through decisively with a 21-0 victory over the Yellow Jackets.

Nobody knew it at the time, but before the decade of the 1940s was over, Butts would be known as the "Bowlmaster." One of the greatest memories of his career came following the Tech defeat in 1941, when he got the news the Orange Bowl wanted his team to visit Miami for its bowl game. Miami officials were trumpeting the notion that Miami's sun, beaches, palms and tropical setting made it the most popular bowl destination this side of Pasadena. Following the shutout of Tech at Grant Field, Butts went up to his suite at the Biltmore Hotel and said softly, "We've been invited to the Orange Bowl." A celebration ensued, and in Athens, when the news got out, people celebrated euphorically. The chapel bell rang into the night.

SCAN TO WATCH

VIDEO FROM 1942

ORANGE BOWL

Sinkwich Shines In Orange Bowl

Jan. 1, 1942 · Georgia 40, Texas Christian 26

With their Orange Bowl invitation, Georgia knew very little about its Southwestern Conference opponent, Texas Christian University. However, the Bulldog coaching staff came into possession of game film of a couple of TCU games. The filming of games had not yet become routinely established, and there was concern about the legality of scouting an opponent via "moving pictures."

Bill Hartman, the backfield coach, remembered that the coaching staff drew the shades and watched the flickering movement of the TCU players on a white bed sheet "in guarded secrecy." The images were without clear definition and so faded that Hartman laughed when he recalled the incident. "You couldn't tell much about what they were doing," he said with a grin.

You would have thought, in retrospect, that the Bulldogs might have had possession of the Horned Frogs' playbook and game plan. The game was so lopsided, 40-7, after three quarters that it led to this assessment by coach Wally Butts: "For the first three quarters, it was the finest offensive display by a Georgia team that I ever saw."

Few backs, even in the later-day offensive era, could ever imagine having a day like that of Frank Sinkwich. The All-American threw three touchdown passes of 15, 61 and 60 yards, ran for a 43-yard score and collected 382 yards in total offense — a record that stood until 2012, 70 years later.

By the fourth quarter, the Bulldogs had become exhausted in the Miami heat, so Butts began putting in substitute players. The Horned Frogs scored three touchdowns late but never had a chance to overtake the Bulldogs.

It didn't go unnoticed that that America was still emotionally overwhelmed by the Dec. 7, 1941, sneak attack on Pearl Harbor by the Japanese. The next season, 1942, would be one to remember, but many of the Georgia players who were playing their last game in Miami, and later Pasadena, would take part in a larger conflict, one that didn't keep the same kind of score — and one where there were no attractive young girls in bathing suits, and bands playing songs like "Chattanooga Choo Choo," and "Don't Sit Under the Apple Tree."

The war's long shadow would encroach across America the following football season, but the heaviest fighting loomed menacingly on the horizon.

Back in Athens, however, the Orange Bowl victory stimulated a memorable celebration. The town loved the Bulldogs and took great pride in the team's success. Georgia's victory over TCU in the Orange Bowl was a milestone achievement.

(Preceding page) After breaking his jaw early in the 1941 season, Frank Sinkwich had the jaw wired, and wore a special helmet to protect it. In the 1942 Orange Bowl against Texas Christian University in Miami, the All-American had 382 yards of total offense, including a 43-yard touchdown run. (Above) In addition to being a great runner, Sinkwich was also an accurate passer and superb punter for the Bulldogs.

A Jewel Of A Comeback

Oct. 31, 1942 · Georgia 21, Alabama 10

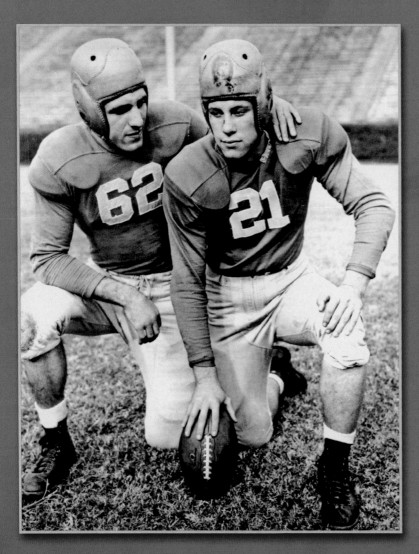

(Left) Charley Trippi, left, and Frank Sinkwich led the Bulldogs to an 11-1 record in 1942. (Opposite page) George Poschner caught two touchdown passes from Sinkwich in the 1942 Alabama game, and was named an All-American after the season.

Coach Wally Butts knew he had a dandy football team when the Bulldogs opened the season in Louisville against Kentucky on Sept. 19, 1942, but the score of that first game, 7-6, gave Georgia's colorful coach the blues. Known as "Weepin' Wally," he moaned the team's shortcomings against Kentucky.

Defeating the Jacksonville Naval Air Station 14-0 the next week in Macon was nothing to write home about, but suddenly the offense began exploding productively, averaging 42.7 points per game for the next seven outings. The season was defined by the 21-10 victory over the Alabama in Atlanta — a jewel of a comeback that brought notable national attention.

Down 10-0 at the end of the third quarter, the Bulldogs scored 21 points in the final period to win 21-10. The contest took place at Georgia Tech's Grant Field because of wartime conditions and gas rationing. Nonetheless, a number of Northern sportswriters journeyed to Atlanta to cover the game, which was in Frank Sinkwich's favor when the votes for the Heisman Trophy were tallied a few weeks later.

Years later, Sinkwich revealed a conversation that took place in the Georgia huddle when the Bulldogs had failed to score for three quarters. "Wouldn't Tommy be proud of us now?" someone said. The reference was to Tommy Witt, a letterman on the 1939 and '40 teams who had lost his life on a bombing mission in North Africa. "That remark seemed to ignite our team," Sinkwich recalled.

Sinkwich himself had a contrasting performance, when you compare the first-half statistics to those of the second half. In the first 30 minutes, the Bulldog tailback completed only 9 of 24 pass attempts. In the final two quarters, he connected on 9 of 13 and two touchdowns. Georgia got its final touchdown when Andy Dudish grabbed a fumble and sprinted in for the score.

The two touchdown passes were to George Poschner, who came to Georgia with Sinkwich and tried out for the team after having been a cheerleader in high school, too small to play football. Poschner made acrobatic catches in the game, which influenced those Northern sportswriters to vote for him for All-America.

On the afternoon, Sinkwich completed 18 of 37 for 231 yards passing. Those numbers reflected the passing emphasis that made Wally Butts the toast of Athens. His teams played exciting football. Nobody in college football exploited the passing game like the Bulldogs.

Sinkwich was on the way to the Heisman Trophy, but not to be overlooked was the fact that his understudy happened to be a versatile tailback named Charley Trippi, who would be heard from before the season was over.

FRANK SINKWICH'S

SCAN TO WATCH

HEISMAN SPEECH

SINKWICH WINS THE HEISMAN

1942

(Left) All-American Frank Sinkwich. (Opposite page) Sinkwich's 1942 Heisman Trophy is on display in the Butts-Mehre Building on the UGA campus.

THE HEISMAN MEMORIAL TROPHY
IS PRESENTED BY
DOWNTOWN ATHLETIC CLUB OF NEW YORK CITY
TO
FRANK SINKWICH
UNIVERSITY OF GEORGIA
AS THE
OUTSTANDING COLLEGE FOOTBALL PLAYER

When the Heisman Trophy votes were tabulated following the 1942 season, Frank Sinkwich was the winner. His photo appeared on the cover of national magazines, causing many out-of-state students to enroll at Georgia.

A handsome, shy and modest native of Youngstown, Ohio, Sinkwich was a reluctant superstar. Sinkwich had enormous pride and he wanted to excel at his favorite game, but national headlines did not turn his head.

There were at least two critical factors in Sinkwich winning the Heisman. One had to do with those Northern sportswriters coming to Atlanta to cover the game with Alabama, in which Sinkwich dazzled those in attendance with his passing performance in the fourth quarter.

The other factor was Sinkwich's courage in playing the 1941 season with a broken jaw. The injury came in the second game with South Carolina in Athens, with Georgia winning 34-6. Georgia's medical staff got the trainer from Tennessee to "build" a face mask to attach to a helmet. Sinkwich pulled down the face bar over his face for protection when he was on the field. He never missed a game.

Even with a broken jaw, opponents could not stop the "Crafty Croatian," who came south from Ohio for adventure, found Athens to his liking, and stayed. Except for a coaching stint after the war, he always lived in the Classic City.

Two memories of mine about Sinkwich are unforgettable.

He once let a friend of mine live in an apartment that he owned and was not using. I walked by an empty bedroom that had no furniture and spotted Frank's Heisman Trophy sitting on the floor. A few years later, I told him about the scene and said that if I had won the Heisman, I'd have it on a pedestal at the entrance to my house.

He said, "It doesn't belong to me. It belongs to the University of Georgia. In fact, I'm thinking of giving it to the school." I went to then-Athletic Director Joel Eaves with the news, and arrangements were made to honor Sinkwich's wishes. Later, the Heisman committee learned of the story and began the practice of awarding two trophies — one to the player and one to his school.

Another time, I asked Sinkwich about his relatives who lived in Croatia. Did he have any interest in going back to where his parents had grown up and meeting his cousins? He said, "No," and explained. "Those folks are Communist aren't they? Well, I am an American and we would not have anything in common."

SCAN TO WATCH

RED BOYD'S

BLOCKED PUNT

A ROSE BOWL VICTORY

Jan. 1, 1943 · Georgia 9, UCLA 0

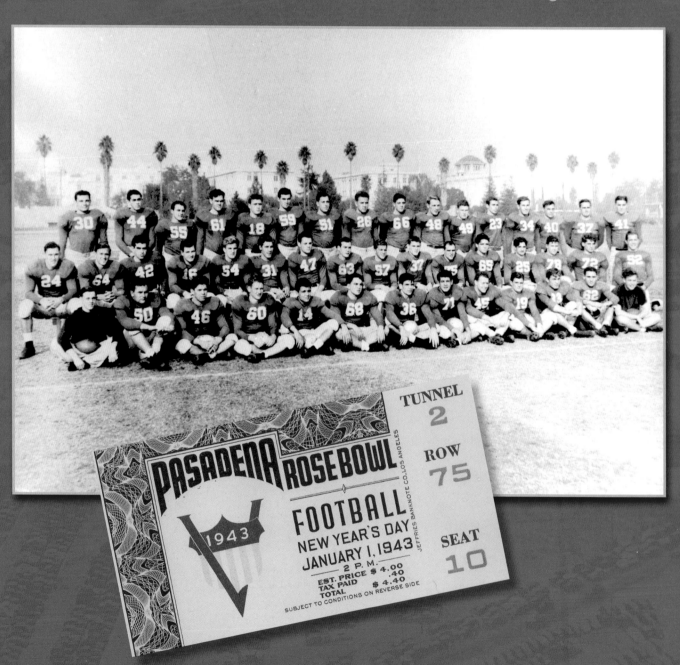

PASADENA ROSE BOWL

1943

FOOTBALL
NEW YEAR'S DAY
JANUARY 1, 1943
2 P.M.
EST. PRICE $ 4.00
TAX PAID $ .40
TOTAL $ 4.40
SUBJECT TO CONDITIONS ON REVERSE SIDE

JEFFRIES BANKNOTE CO., LOS ANGELES

TUNNEL
2

ROW
75

SEAT
10

ating back to the 1930s, Georgia has traditionally played Georgia Tech on the Saturday after Thanksgiving. There have been some consequential games in the rivalry, especially when Tech was a member of the Southeastern Conference.

But none was more significant in the ancient series than the one played in Athens on Nov. 28, 1942. Tech was undefeated and Georgia was once beaten. The Rose Bowl announced that the winner of the game would be invited to Pasadena.

The previous week, the Bulldogs, who were ranked No. 1, were upset by Auburn in Columbus. Experiencing a letdown that cost them dearly, the Bulldogs came home from Auburn smarting from the 27-13 loss.

Many players on the team knew coach Wally Butts' ire would be reserved for them the next week, but when they reflected back on the Tech game, they were appreciative that their coach had them primed for a peak game in the regular-season finale. It was no contest, with the Bulldogs beating Tech handily 34-0.

(Preceding page) The 1943 Rose Bowl champions posed for a photo while in Pasadena. (Right) Red Boyd blocks a punt by UCLA's Bob Waterfield for a safety. Photo courtesy of the L.A. Times. (Below) An aerial view of the 1943 Rose Bowl.

California here we come!

Georgia stayed at the Huntington Hotel and enjoyed the West Coast experience, which they, otherwise, could only have dreamed about. Comedian Joe E. Brown showed up for practice. They met movie stars like Bob Hope, Susan Hayward, Mickey Rooney and Ava Gardner. Coach Butts worried about all the distractions that might take his Bulldogs' minds off the game. The Bulldogs were highly favored over UCLA, led by tailback Bob Waterfield — who would eventually be elected to the Pro Football Hall of Fame, but who was perhaps most remembered by his marriage to buxom movie star Jane Russell.

The game featured Georgia's Charley Trippi rushing 27 times for 115 yards to become the game's outstanding player, as the Bulldogs moved the ball up and down the field but not scoring a touchdown.

Finally, in the fourth quarter, Red Boyd, a mountaineer farm boy from Toccoa, blocked a Waterfield punt out of the UCLA end zone for a safety, which, as it turned out, would have been enough points to win the game. Later, following an interception, Georgia moved down to the 1-yard line, where Butts sent Frank Sinkwich into the game to score the only touchdown that enabled the Bulldogs to defeat UCLA 9-0.

With both Sinkwich and Trippi being first-generation Americans and Boyd, a country boy who probably never returned to California, you have to bring to the forefront that oft-used slogan, "Only in America." College football has often made us think about that phrase.

(Preceding page) Frank Sinkwich autographs a football in Pasadena. (Below) The Bulldogs spend some quality time with actress Susan Hayward in California.

CHARLEY TRIPPI'S PUNT RETURN

SCAN TO WATCH

TRIPPI'S GREAT RETURN

Jan. 1, 1946 · Georgia 20, Tulsa 6

(Left) Charley Trippi returned from military duty in time for the fifth game of the 1945 season and helped the Bulldogs earn an invitation to the 1946 Oil Bowl (Opposite page) Trippi on the run against Tulsa in the Oil Bowl.

In 1945, good news was flashing around the world. World War II was coming to a close. On May 7, it was V-E Day (victory in Europe), and victory in Japan came when the Japanese capitulated (V-J Day) on Aug. 14, although formal surrender would take place on Sept. 2.

In Athens, Georgia was getting ready for another football season after having fielded motley teams in 1943 and '44, made up mostly of players either too young for the draft or who had been declared 4-F.

Even with a dropoff in talent, coach Wallace Butts was able to field winning teams against competition like Presbyterian, which Georgia played twice in Athens, Daniel Field (the Bulldogs lost that one 18-7), Howard, VMI, Tennessee Tech and Wake Forest. In 1943, the Bulldogs played LSU in Baton Rouge and Columbus, and lost both times. The Tigers were led by their great back Steve Van Buren, who would lead the Philadelphia Eagles to NFL titles in 1948 and '49.

In 1944, the Bulldogs went 7-3, with the war years revealing that Butts found a way to win even if he did not have any big stars on his team. The Bulldogs would rebound in 1945, as players returned from the military — like Charley Trippi, who

arrived in Athens from the Air Force for the fifth game versus LSU.

The Bulldogs were undefeated when the Tigers lined up between the hedges on Oct. 20. All the headlines belonged to Trippi, but not after the game, as LSU thrashed the home team 32-0.

The story of the game had to do with the new system Butts had put in: the T-formation. Trippi, even for the military teams he played with in the Air Force, had always been a single-wing tailback. Now he was operating in the "T" from the left halfback position.

Following the LSU debacle, Georgia lost 28-14 the next week to Alabama in Birmingham. But the Bulldogs would not lose again, winning five consecutive games for a 9-2 record. That included a 20-6 victory over Tulsa in the Oil Bowl in Houston on New Year's Day 1946.

Trippi had returned, the Bulldogs had gone bowling, and the war was over. Everybody talked about Trippi's great punt return in the Oil Bowl. There was no television, but newspaper accounts sang Trippi's praises, with many observers claiming it was the greatest punt return of all time. Judge for yourself by watching the video embedded on the preceding page.

Trippi Leads Dogs To Perfect Record

Nov. 2, 1946 · Georgia 14, Alabama 0

(Left) In 2012, Charley Trippi, right, received a copy of his 1946 Maxwell Award from Executive Director Mark Wolpert. (Opposite page) Trippi turns upfield against Alabama in 1946.

Following the 1945 season, Charley Trippi could have moved on to the National Football League. His time spent in the Air Force made him eligible for the draft.

At the conclusion of the Oil Bowl game in January 1946, Trippi's teammate John Donaldson remembered coach Wally Butts' emotional outburst in the locker room, pleading with Trippi to return for his final year of eligibility. He even announced that Trippi would be captain of the 1946 team. Butts was taking no chances.

Trippi did return, and what a year he had! He led the Bulldogs to an undefeated season, as the team averaged 37.2 points per game and scored less than 30 points only twice: 28 versus Kentucky and 14 against Alabama.

The Alabama game was a classic between the hedges, with the Bulldogs winning 14-0 over the defending national champions. The Tide's star player was Harry Gilmer, the top passer in college football, who went 0 for 8 against UGA. Lurking from his safety position, Trippi made sure that Gilmer would not hurt the Bulldogs through the air.

In the first quarter, Trippi threw for a touchdown to end Dan Edwards. Then, early in the second quarter, Trippi, a driven competitor, demonstrated why he was such an outstanding performer. Trippi, one of the finest punters in college football, tried a quick-kick, which was blocked by Alabama. Trippi then wheeled around and outran the Alabama players chasing the bounding ball, dove into a pile and came up with the ball at the Georgia 1-yard line.

Then, on fourth down, Trippi was not through. He punted over the head of the Alabama safety, which resulted in decent field position for the Bulldogs, who avoided a potential game-changing scoring opportunity for Alabama.

In the Sugar Bowl on New Year's Day 1947, Trippi again was the big star, leading the Bulldogs to a 20-10 victory over a North Carolina team led by Charlie "Choo-Choo" Justice. Trippi played the

entire 60 minutes and threw a 67-yard touchdown pass to Dan Edwards, which remained the Sugar Bowl record for many years.

Trippi left Georgia for the NFL with these impressive stats in only two-and-a-half years of varsity football: 1,669 yards rushing (6.4 average) and 32 touchdowns, along with 1,566 passing yards. In addition to being the team's punter, nobody was a more feared kick returner than Trippi, which is why history is on the side of anybody who believes Trippi is Georgia's greatest all-around player. Georgia Tech's Bobby Dodd was among the many who saw Trippi play, and he said Trippi was the greatest player he ever saw.

UGA ARRIVES ON THE SCENE

1956

(Left) This bulldog became the Georgia mascot in 1956. Since then, Sonny and Cecelia Seiler have provided the Ugas for UGA.

(Far left) Coach Wally Butts with a collection of helmets in the 1950s. The Butts family cared for the pre-Uga mascot named Mike. (Opposite page) Butts agreed that the Seilers' bulldog should be used as the new Georgia mascot.

Until 1956, Georgia's mascots were "volunteer" Bulldogs, walk-on mascots, if you will. One of the last of the mascots — before the Uga dynasty — was Mike, a brindled bulldog that was owned by C.L. Fain but pretty much adopted by coach Wally Butts.

Mike lived at the old Field House, which is where the Rankin Smith Center stands today. When Mike died, sadness enveloped the Butts household, but there was not much fuss about it made in the papers. No search for a replacement was bandied about in the press, but Dan Magill — ever in tune with the importance of Georgia traditions — knew that Cecelia Seiler, wife of Sonny Seiler, a Bulldog swimmer who worked part time in the ticket office while studying for a law degree, had been given a wedding present of a bulldog by a friend, Frank Heard of Columbus.

Magill recommended to Butts that the Seilers' bulldog be used as the Georgia mascot. Butts agreed and invited Sonny up to his office in old Stegeman Hall to make it official.

From that point forward — from the opening game with Florida State in 1956 until today — the Seilers have owned, bred and cared for the Ugas. Also from the beginning, the Ugas have been all-white, male English bulldogs. Cecilia made the red jerseys with a block-lettered black Georgia "G" in the beginning, and that tradition has remained. You seldom see Uga without his block-lettered "G," although in recent years the Nike swoosh has appeared on a sleeve of the jersey, just as it does on those of the players.

The Seilers, who have maintained the Ugas with love and devotion, have made a wonderful contribution to an important UGA tradition. Uga never misses a game and was deemed the No. 1 mascot in college football by *Sports Illustrated* in 1997. Uga has appeared at the Heisman Trophy banquet (in a tux no less), the movie "Midnight in the Garden of Good and Evil," and at the U.S. Capitol Building in

Washington, D.C. Everywhere Uga goes, he is treated like a rock star.

Many have assumed that Georgia's ties with Yale influenced the Bulldog nickname, but that is not accurate. Following a tie with Virginia in Charlottesville, when Georgia was fighting for the Southern Conference title, *Atlanta Constitution* writer Cliff Wheatley frequently referred to the heart and tenacity of the "bulldogs" at least five times. The nickname then gained traction, and you know the rest of the story.

At the beginning of the 2012 season, Sonny Seiler announced that Russ, the reserve masscot, officially became Uga IX.

THERON SAPP'S
SCAN TO WATCH
TOUCHDOWN

DOGS END TECH'S WINNING STREAK

Nov. 30, 1957 · Georgia 7, Georgia Tech 0

(Left) Theron Sapp scores the winning touchdown against Georgia Tech in 1957. It ended a losing streak to Tech dating back to 1949. (Opposite page) Coach Wally Butts and his coaches have a little fun in the locker room.

EAST STAND
GATE **5**
AISLE **12**
SEC. **22**
ROW **30**
SEAT **15**
ADM. $5.00
NOV. 30, 1957

GEORGIA TECH
VERSUS
GEORG

1957
SATURDAY
2:00 P.M. E.S.T. · NOV. 30

HOLD YOUR OWN TICKET   NO REFUND

The 1950s were not kind to Wallace Butts. After imposing success in the '40s, The Little Round Man of Georgia football fell on hard times. Some say his Spartan style of coaching became a recruiting deterrent. He didn't win as many games, for whatever reasons, and the bowl tradition, which he established in his first decade of coaching, went dormant.

Others thought his penchant for the passing game put him at a disadvantage. Most coaches of that era held the conviction that a running game and sound defense were the best way to win games. On top of that, the college rules changed in 1954. Players had to compete on both sides of the ball. Limited substitution became the norm.

Without question, he was the victim of tough luck — especially against Georgia Tech, which began a winning streak in 1949 that lasted through 1956. An example of the hard-luck sentiment came in 1954 when, in the rain and mud in Athens, Georgia held a 3-0 lead at the half and had the option to kick or receive. The Bulldogs had moved up and down the field in the first half, seemingly at will, but scored no touchdowns. His players lobbied hard for Butts to elect to receive to begin the second half. He yielded, not a high-percentage decision under the circumstances. On the first play following the kickoff, Georgia fumbled, Tech recovered and threw a touchdown pass to make it 7-3. That ended the scoring and left Georgia with a bitter defeat.

The Bulldogs could not stop the bleeding until a bit-

ter cold day on Grant Field, Nov. 30, 1957. It was a hard-fought game, with Georgia determined to break the drought but Tech stood fast, refusing to yield. Late in the fourth quarter, Tech fumbled near midfield and Theron Sapp, from his linebacker position on defense, recovered.

Facing a third-and-12 situation on the ensuing possession, Charley Britt completed a pass to Jimmy Orr for a first down to keep the drive moving. When the Bulldogs got to the Tech goal line, the Jacket defense stiffened. On third down, Britt tried a quarterback sneak but couldn't get in. In the huddle, the players were saying, "Give it to Sapp." On fourth down, Sapp, who recovered from a broken neck in high school to return to football, blasted through the Tech defensive left side, clear out of the end zone, getting blocking help from Cicero Lucas, Nat Dye, Ken Cooper and Jimmy Orr.

"We were not going to be denied," Sapp said.

SCAN TO WATCH THE WINNING PLAY VS. AUBURN

TARKENTON DRAWS UP A WIN

Nov. 14, 1959 · Georgia 14, Auburn 13

(Left) Fran Tarkenton was a local star while playing for Athens High School. (Opposite page) Tarkenton on the run.

After breaking the drought against Georgia Tech in 1957, there was a new optimism about the Bulldog football team. Georgia had defeated Tech again in 1958. There was a group of young sophomores, led by quarterback Fran Tarkenton and guard Pat Dye, who believed they could win.

J.B. Whitworth, who was head coach Wally Butts' line coach in the 1940s — a time of plenty in Athens — returned to join his old coach. While he underscored discipline, Whitworth had a seasoned ability to establish rapport with the players, who will tell you today that he brought a new attitude to Athens.

Limited substitution rules still prevailed, but Butts and his staff developed two teams that played equally: Charley Britt's team and Tarkenton's team.

The Bulldogs started fast in 1959, defeating a good Alabama team 17-3 in the opener between the hedges. Georgia would lose only one time during the season, on an "off day" against South Carolina in Columbia, 30-14. The Bulldogs would defeat their main rivals — Florida, Auburn and Georgia Tech — to win a fourth Southeastern Conference title for Butts. The highlight came when the Dogs nipped Auburn 14-13 in Athens.

It was a defensive battle much of the afternoon, with Auburn taking a 6-0 first-half lead on two field goals. Bulldog punter Bobby Walden kept the visitors backed up throughout the second half, setting up a field-position advantage for Georgia when he kicked a 45-yarder out of bounds at the Auburn 2. Soon afterward, Britt returned a punt, zigzagging his way through the Auburn defense for a 39-yard touchdown to put Georgia up 7-6.

Twelve plays later, Britt, from his "searchlight" position in punt formation, backed into Walden's kick, which Auburn recovered at the Georgia 1-yard line. The Tigers scored and went back ahead 13-7. It didn't look good for the home team, but with less than three minutes on the clock, end Bill Herron forced a fumble, which Pat Dye recovered at the Auburn 35.

The cogent Tarkenton then took over, passing for 16 and 9 yards to Don Soberdash, and Georgia had the ball just outside the Auburn 10-yard line, needing a touchdown to win. It appeared that Auburn's defense would not yield, but on fourth down and 13, Tarkenton drew up a play in the weathered turf and then threw a touchdown pass to Herron.

"Payoff pitch and pandemonium," is the way Dan Magill described it.

Durward Pennington's extra point gave Georgia a 14-13 victory and the SEC championship. The Bulldogs went on to beat Missouri 14-0 in the Orange Bowl on Jan. 1, 1960.

(Below) Tarkenton with coach Wally Butts and teammate Pat Dye. (Right) The Bulldogs prepare to fly to the Orange Bowl, where they beat Missouri 14-0.

DOOLEY TAKES THE HELM

December 1963

(Left) While being carried off the field by his players, new Georgia coach Vince Dooley receives congratulations from Georgia Tech coach Bobby Dodd after the Bulldogs beat the Yellow Jackets 7-0 in 1964. (Opposite page) Georgia quarterback Preston Ridlehuber avoids a Texas Tech defender in the 1964 Sun Bowl. His pass to Fred Barber set up the touchdown for the 7-0 win.

By 1963, Vince Dooley, a former Auburn quarterback, had become the Tigers' freshman coach. After graduation from Auburn in 1954, Dooley entered the Marines as an officer and returned to his alma mater as an assistant coach.

His early responsibilities included scouting Auburn opponents with Joel Eaves — who, in addition to coaching basketball, was a football assistant and scouting coordinator. Eaves and Dooley traveled to many games together, scouting the designated opposition. Eaves, who had coached Dooley in basketball and learned about his cool-under-fire temperament, was convinced that his protégé would be a successful head coach. As a scout, he further became aware of Dooley's knowledge of the game and his appreciation for sound, fundamental football.

However, when Eaves became Georgia's athletic director in 1963, he initially worried that Dooley, at age 31, was perhaps too young to take over a head-coaching position at a major college. Eaves explored other possibilities but settled on Dooley, much to the shock of the Bulldog fan base. They were expecting a coach with an established reputation. Few had ever heard of Vince Dooley, prompting the epithet, "Vince who?" The immediate reaction to the news was less than favorable. "The Auburn freshman coach is now coach of the Bulldogs?"

People were expecting the worst, but Eaves' clairvoyance brought about one of the truly great decisions for Georgia athletics.

Dooley would become Georgia's winningest coach, with six Southeastern Conference titles and

the 1980 national championship highlighting his resume. "Vince, Who?" would become the toast of the state.

His first team went 7-3-1, beating Texas Tech in the Sun Bowl. A 7-0 victory over Georgia Tech bought about a lot of confidence in the new staff. Georgia fans were overwhelmed by the attitude and hustle of the Bulldog players, who were hungry to win.

In 1965, Dooley recruited one of the best freshman classes of his tenure, a prized group that included Jake Scott and Bill Stanfill, who have been elected to the College Football Hall of Fame, and Billy Payne, who would bring the 1996 Olympics to Atlanta and become chairman of the Augusta

National Golf Club. His greatest player, Herschel Walker, led Georgia to the national championship in 1980 and to three straight SEC titles.

Dooley is a member of the College Football Hall of Fame and was Georgia athletic director from 1979-2004. His vision and leadership upgraded sports teams and facilities to championship levels. Under his leadership, Georgia had one of the best all-around athletic programs in the country.

(Below) The 1964 Alabama game, which the sixth-ranked Crimson Tide won 31-3 en route to the national championship, was a good learning experience for Dooley's young Bulldogs. (Opposite page, top) By 1965 when this photo was taken, Dooley had already built a winning foundation in Athens. (Opposite page, bottom) A commemorative football from the Sun Bowl victory over Texas Tech.

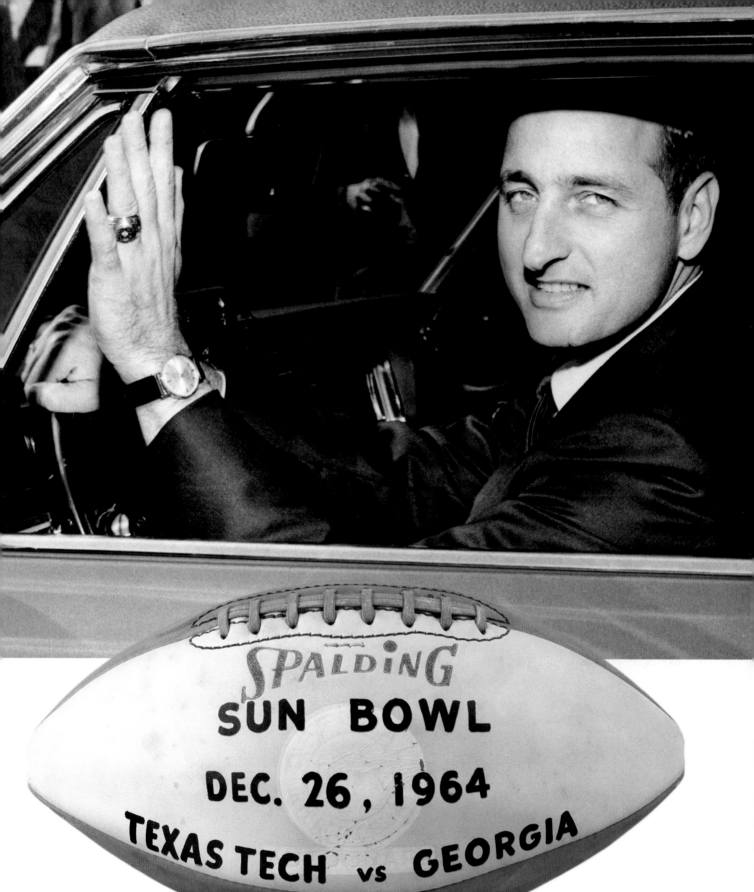

Flea-Flicker Beats National Champs

Sept. 18, 1965 · Georgia 18, Alabama 17

PHOTO BY
BILLY DOWNS
ATLANTA

Following the serendipitous season of 1964, and with a plethora of talented and seasoned players returning, Georgia had reason for optimism for the 1965 season. Injuries, however, riddled the team and caused a downturn in the last half of the season that caused the Bulldogs to struggle, losing four of five games by Thanksgiving.

Two days after the holiday, however, the Bulldogs defeated Georgia Tech 17-7 in Atlanta and enabled the Red and Black to finish 6-4. Unfortunately, no bowl opportunity awaited this capable team.

To appreciate "what might have been," you only have to hark back to the opening game with Alabama, the defending national champions. NBC was on hand with Jim Simpson and Bud Wilkinson announcing the game, which was significant in that Wilkinson — the former Oklahoma head coach — gained a great impression of Vince Dooley as a football coach. His favorable assessment would cause Oklahoma to try to hire the Georgia coach a few months later.

Georgia outplayed the Tide in the first half, taking a 10-3 lead, highlighted by George Patton's touchdown after catching a fumble in mid-air. In the second half, Alabama tightened things up, aided by a fumble at the Georgia 29, and scored to tie the game. Alabama went ahead 17-10 late in the fourth quarter on a Steve Sloan touchdown from 2 yards out.

Bulldog partisans were downcast, but immediately after the ensuing kickoff, Dooley sent in word to run the "flea-flicker." Kirby Moore, the quarterback, was flummoxed but followed orders. A native of Dothan, Alabama, Moore was playing in his first varsity game. He threw a short out pass to a button-hooking Pat Hodgson, who had to lean back to grab the ball. Hodgson caught it, and with one sweeping motion, shoveled a lateral into the arms of Bob Taylor, who

(Preceding page) Coach Vince Dooley leans forward to shake hands with Alabama coach Paul "Bear" Bryant after the Bulldogs upset the defending national champions 18-17 in 1965. (Left) The "flea-flicker" that beat the Crimson Tide was captured on film. The play covered 73 yards. It was Alabama's only loss of the season.

QB Kirby Moore passes...

...to TE Pat Hodgson...

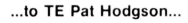

...to Bob Taylor...

...who scores on 73-yd TD.

...who pitches back...

(Above) When the 1965 season was over, Coach Dooley turned down a lucrative offer from Oklahoma to become their next head coach.

sped past the shocked Alabama defense for a 73-yard play that set Sanford Stadium into a frenzy.

The game was not over, however, as the Bulldogs called timeout on the sideline to discuss which play to run. This is where Wilkinson, now on the sideline, gained a favorable appraisal about the calm and collected Dooley. There was no question about going for two — just a matter of which play. Moore rolled to his right and calmly threw to Hodgson for the two points and one of the biggest upsets in Sanford Stadium history.

Later, no sooner than a 90-day note would become due, big bucks and big oil would tempt the Bulldogs' youthful head coach. But Dooley would spurn Oklahoma's offer at the end of the season to remain with the Bulldogs, which stimulated the ringing of the chapel bell.

Bulldogs Surprise
Rose Bowl Champs

Oct. 2, 1965 · Georgia 15, Michigan 7

(Above) Georgia's Bobby Etter kicked three field goals to help beat Michigan on their home turf. (Opposite page) Erk Russell's defense allowed only one touchdown against the defending Rose Bowl champions.

Big Ten Conference & Rose Bowl Champs

MICHIGAN

GEORGIA

Saturday 1965
Oct. 2—1:30 p.m.

Captain
TOM CECCHINI

SEC.	ROW	SEAT
1	19	22

MICHIGAN STADIUM

Georgia's upset of Alabama in 1965's opening game was followed by a 24-10 victory over Vanderbilt, which gave the Bulldogs a 2-0 record when they made the trip to Ann Arbor, Michigan, for a game with the defending Rose Bowl champions.

Georgia's upset of Alabama was a big deal in the Southeastern Conference, but it didn't impress the rank and file in Ann Arbor. There was a "ho-hum" attitude on campus, one in which the Bulldogs were being taken for granted. There was more interest in the first Big Ten game on Michigan's schedule the following Saturday when Michigan State was the next opponent. Fewer than 60,000 showed up in the 103,000-plus-seat stadium for the Georgia game.

Everything accommodated the underdog circumstance for Georgia. Hail to the victor? It would not be Michigan. Glory to Old Georgia was the theme at the end of the game, when the upstart Bulldogs came away with a 15-7 victory.

In the first half, Georgia scored on two field goals by Bobby Etter, but Michigan led 7-6 at intermission.

The second half pretty much belonged to the visitors from the South, as quarterback Preston Ridle-huber managed the game superbly against a big and powerful Michigan defensive line. The Bulldogs scored nine points while the defense kept the Wolverines from scoring again.

Ridlehuber directed a 51-yard dive in the fourth quarter, gaining 22 yards by running to his right and reversing his field to come up with a big gain. He threw 10 yards to Pat Hodgson for the touchdown. A two-point conversion pass to Stu Mosher failed. Later, a Etter field goal of 31 yards sealed the victory.

It was a happy band of overachievers who boarded a couple of Southern Airways Martin 404s, which had to refuel along the way, arriving in Athens near midnight. It appeared that half the town had crowded its way to Ben Epps Field to greet their returning heroes. It was the largest crowd ever to greet a Georgia team arriving home following victory.

As the planes banked to land from the East, you could see headlights on cars for miles. The highways and the airport were jammed with fans wanting to congratulate the victorious Bulldogs. It ranks today as Athens' greatest traffic jam.

You would have thought that Georgia had reversed the results of the Civil War. It was that kind of day.

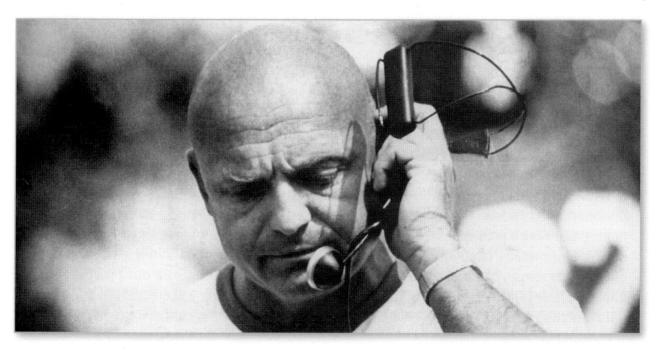

Dooley's First SEC Title

Nov. 12, 1966 · Georgia 21, Auburn 13

(Above) Brad Johnson fights for extra yardage to score against Auburn in 1966. The 21-13 victory gave coach Vince Dooley his first of six Southeastern Conference titles, and it came against his alma mater on the field where he had starred as quarterback.

The freshman class Vince Dooley and his staff recruited in 1965 were precocious sophomores in 1966. They had gotten the varsity's attention in scrimmages during the previous fall. They were upstart and tenacious. In several of the practice-field game-style scrimmages, the freshmen were declared the victors.

On defense, you noted that tackle Bill Stanfill was like the long arm of the law, reaching out to yank down any runner who came his way. Jake Scott's slashing style resulted in big plays, as he ran people down with an uncommon relentlessness, made one-handed interceptions, made crisp tackles that left welts and bruised runners who came his way. Happy Dicks, cogent and workmanlike, belonged to the linebacker intelligentsia.

There was Kent Lawrence with sprinter's speed for varied offensive assignments and kick returning. Brad Johnson, a productive fullback — whose hallmark was superior blocking expertise — was a fine runner. Billy Payne, the ultimate overachiever who arrived as a quarterback and turned into a receiver, later made All-SEC as a defensive end. They blended fluidly with upperclassmen like Tommy Lawhorne, George Patton, Hardy King, Edgar Chandler and Frank Richter.

In 1966, the Bulldogs would win the first of Dooley's six Southeastern Conference championships, with the only loss coming in Miami, 7-6, in the Orange Bowl when mistakes plagued the offense. A bad snap kept Bobby Etter from converting a third field goal, which might have won the game.

Undefeated in conference play, Georgia played Auburn on a muddy field. The soggy track didn't seem to bother the home team, as Auburn quarterback Loran Carter ran for a score of 36 yards and passed to Freddie Hyatt for a 31-yard touchdown in the first half. An all-out rush forced the point-after kick to go wide, and Auburn led 13-0 at the half.

The second half was all Georgia. The first touchdown came on a 67-yard drive, featuring the "Great Mudder," Brad Johnson, who ran for 24 yards and then followed that with a 7-yard touchdown run. The Bulldogs were now trailing 13-7. Two more scores would be added — a 52-yard pass from Kirby Moore to Hardy King, and an insurance touchdown when Ronnie Jenkins scored from 4 yards out late in the fourth quarter.

The Bulldogs gave Dooley his first SEC championship ride — a memorable one in that it gave him that first title and against his alma mater on the field where he had starred as a quarterback for Auburn.

67

Scott Shines In Return

Sept. 14, 1968 · Georgia 17, Tennessee 17

(Above) Jake Scott streaks down the sideline on his 90-yard punt return for a touchdown against Tennessee in 1968. (Opposite
page) The 1968 Bulldogs won the SEC title
and finished No. 1 in one poll.

35th Annual
Sugar Bowl Classic

· Auspices ·
New Orleans
Mid-Winter
Sports
Association

TULANE
SUGAR
BOWL
STADIUM

Wed., January 1st.
1969

Kick-off 1:00 P. M.

WEST STAND
RAMP   4
SEC.   H
ROW   18
SEAT   11

PRICE
$6.50
Tax Included

...ONSIBLE FOR LOST, STOLEN, MISPLACED TICKETS · HOLD YOUR OWN TICKET · NO REFUND · SEE CONDITIONS ON BACK

In 1967, the Georgia team began with high hopes but lost to Archie Manning and Ole Miss in Jackson and to Houston in the Astrodome 14-13. Florida also won a close one in Jacksonville, 17-16.

Jake Scott had been declared academically ineligible for the '67 season. The coaches felt that he might have been the difference in at least a couple of those games.

Scott would return to the lineup in 1968, and his impact was quickly confirmed. He made plays like it was as easy as sending a dog to fetch a stick — in the brush, into a stream, wherever. In the opening game with No. 9 Tennessee, the defending SEC champions, on its new Tartan turf and a with new rule — stopping the clock after a first down — Scott had a one-handed interception, a leaping stab that made Bud Wilkinson, the former Oklahoma coach doing color for ABC TV, almost leap out of the broadcast booth. Wilkinson then waxed admiringly when, late in the third quarter, Scott fielded a punt at his 10-yard line and streaked down the sideline in front of the Georgia bench for a touchdown to give the Dogs a 10-7 lead.

As Scott gained the advantage and began to distance himself from the chasing Volunteers, about the

35-yard line, a Georgia helmet rolled out onto the field. Those who saw it were aghast. The helmet was right in Scott's path, the two almost converging simultaneously. Scott hopped over the helmet effortlessly. The helmet belonged to lineman George White, who was quite chagrined. With no harm done, he good-naturedly accepted the kidding by his teammates.

Later, White explained what happened. "As I moved up to the sideline to watch Jake's run, other players began to crowd in around those who were nearest the sideline. Somebody bumped into me from behind and knocked my helmet loose from my grasp. I was in misery until I saw Jake hop over the helmet and sprint on into the end zone for the touchdown."

Later in the fourth quarter, broad-shouldered Bruce Kemp thundered off tackle and dashed 80 yards for a touchdown and a 17-9 lead. With the advent of the new clock rule, Tennessee was able to gain a tie by scoring a touchdown and a two-point conversion with time running out.

The Bulldogs had one other tie, 10-10 versus Houston in Athens, but won the rest of their games, captured the SEC title and were ranked No. 1 in the Litkenhous Poll.

DOGS RALLY TO STUN VOLS

Nov. 3, 1973 · Georgia 35, Tennessee 31

(Left) Coach Vince Dooley with several of his players from the 1973 squad that went 7-4-1, with beating Tennessee being the regular-season highlight. Standing are, from left to right, Horace King, Dooley, Andy Johnson and John Duke, and kneeling are Rusty Russell, Clarence Pope and Richard Appleby. (Opposite page, bottom) Quarterback Andy Johnson, pictured here against Auburn, scored the winning touchdown against the Vols. (Opposite page, top) Dooley smiles after being presented the Peach Bowl trophy after beating Maryland.

Georgia returned to Knoxville in 1973 for the first time since the debut of the Tartan turf. The '70s were up-and-down years for Vince Dooley's Dogs, and winning consistently was a challenge, except in 1976 when the Bulldogs won the SEC championship behind quarterback Ray Goff. A bitter loss to Auburn in 1971 in Athens kept Andy Johnson from leading the Bulldogs to an SEC title.

After 1971, results can best be described as "so-so" for the Dogs. They went 7-4 in 1972, but did not earn a bowl invitation, and 7-4-1 in 1973, defeating Maryland 17-16 in a Peach Bowl thriller. Georgia Tech was a 10-3 victim in 1973.

But the game in '73 that warmed Bulldog hearts came in Knoxville, where Georgia visited for the first time since 1968. After having been embarrassed by Vanderbilt and Kentucky, nobody would have expected the Bulldogs to make much noise in Knoxville, where over 100,000 fans gathered for the game.

The final score: Georgia 35, Tennessee 31. But how the game was won will always remain a highlight with Bulldog partisans. The first half represented "Dooley Ball" at its finest. Although down twice, 7-0 and 14-7, Georgia rallied with toe-to-toe scoring drives of 81, 70 and 43 yards to lead 21-14 at the half. Interestingly, the Bulldogs did not complete a single pass on those drives.

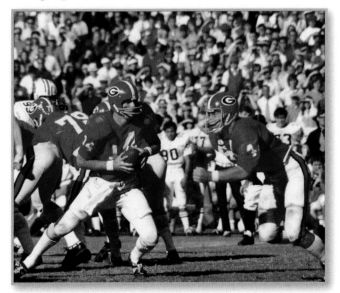

Tennessee dominated the third quarter by scoring 17 unanswered points, and it appeared that the Georgia offense had lost its firepower. Trailing 31-21, a renewed energy surfaced with 10:45 remaining on the clock, when Abb Ansley intercepted a Vol pass at the Georgia 21. Johnson then led his team on a 14-play, 79-yard drive that culminated with a 6-yard pass to Jimmy Poulas. After Alan Leavitt's point-after kick, the Bulldogs closed within 31-28.

As the final quarter began to reach its conclusion, Tennessee, in punt formation at its own 28, elected to fake punt. Ric Reider led the defensive charge, aided by Bubba Wilson, and threw the Vol fullback for a 2-yard loss. In five plays, Georgia was in the end zone, getting an assist from the hardpan Tartan turf. When Andy Johnson "reached" the ball to running back Glynn Harrison, it hit his hip but bounded perfectly into the quarterback's hands, and he scored around left end from 8 yards out — as the Tennessee fans looked at the final score in disbelief.

THE WINNING

SCAN TO WATCH

PLAY VS FLORIDA

JUNKYARD DOGS
TRICK GATORS

Nov. 8, 1975 · Georgia 10, Florida 7

(Above) The Georgia fans start celebrating while the Bulldogs count off the final seconds against Florida in 1975.

vs **Florida**
JACKSONVILLE, FLA., THE GATOR BOWL · NOVEMBER 8, 1975 · ONE DOLLAR

(Above) Tight end Richard Appleby prepares to throw a 55-yard touchdown pass to flanker Gene Washington (above left) to beat the Gators 10-7.

There are many unforgettable moments for every campus that hosts football competition. Some go against you, and those wearing opposing colors get to celebrate the spoils of success. It's part of the game and is what makes college football so great.

In 1975, Georgia fielded a team known as the Junkyard Dogs. The previous season, the Bulldogs had hired Bill Pace, a highly regarded offensive coach, to install the veer option, and the new offense was gaining momentum. The '75 Dogs could put points on the scoreboard, and the defense had improved dramatically from the 1974 season, when it gave up 31 points or more five times. However, nobody thought Georgia could play with Florida. The Gators arrived in Jacksonville with a team averaging 433.5 yards and 29.0 points per outing.

Florida ran the wishbone but had ingeniously added multiple passing plays, which became labeled the "Broken Bone." The Gators jumped out front early when Georgia fumbled the ball to Florida at the Bulldogs' 44-yard line. Eleven plays later, the boys from Gainesville were on the scoreboard with a 7-0 lead.

You could have won a lot of money at that point if you had wagered that the scoring by Florida had concluded for the day. Not even Erk Russell would

have bet on that. From that point on, the Gators — although gaining 232 yards rushing and 382 yards total offense — never scored again.

Meanwhile, the Bulldogs threatened but could not score except for a field goal by Allan Leavitt near the end of the first half, as Florida left the field with a 7-3 lead.

The two teams played to a stalemate in the third and fourth quarters, but with 2:24 left on the clock, Pace called for a special play — he always had one in his repertoire — the end-around pass. Tight end Richard Appleby got the pitchout from quarterback Matt Robinson and headed around right end, as the Florida defense flowed in his direction. Appleby abruptly pulled up and heaved a long bomb past the Florida secondary to sprinter Gene Washington for a touchdown and a 10-7 victory.

After the game, I interviewed Appleby and asked him if he was nervous when Pace told him the plan. "I guess you could say I was a little bit nervous," he said while grinning broadly, "but you can say I rose to the occasion." That is one of the classic quotes in Bulldog football history.

ANOTHER SEC CHAMPIONSHIP

1976

(Left) Quarterback Ray Goff is off and running against Vanderbilt in 1976. Goff was named the SEC Player of the Year. (Opposite page, top) Defensive coordinator Erk Russell, pictured with two of his Bulldogs, played a big role in Georgia winning the SEC in 1976. (Opposite page, bottom) Goff was one of the most effective running quarterbacks in college football.

Following surprising success in 1975, Georgia had gotten settled with the veer offense. Quarterbacks Matt Robinson and Ray Goff were co-equals when Bill Pace put in the veer in 1974, but Robinson was injured early on and Goff got the lion's share of playing time. Goff became one of the most effective and ravaging quarterback runners in football. Interestingly, he had come to Athens from Moultrie, where he was recognized for setting countless records as a passer.

At 6-foot-2 and 201 pounds, Goff had good speed, but what made him so successful on the option was that he developed state-of-the-art timing for the veer. First of all, his production was aided by a very capable and stud-like offense line, led by Mike Wilson and Steve Collier at tackle, Joel Parish and George Collins at guard, and Joe Tereshinski at center. There were running lanes, but at some point out on the corner, the quarterback is on his own. This is where Goff became a master of the option pitch. He had big hands and could grasp the football like it was a loaf of bread. When he reached the corner and optioned the end, he usually was at full speed. There was always a trailing back, and the defense had difficulty reacting to Goff's moves. If the defense closed down on him, he would pitch to the trail back. If

there was any hesitation, Goff would cut inside and turn upfield. He made a lot of first downs with his quickness and canny judgment on whether to pitch or keep the ball.

The Bulldogs had one lapse, against Ole Miss in Oxford when the Rebels, coached by a former Georgia end Ken Cooper, were opportunistic and won 21-17 in an upset.

Rebounding from the disappointment in Oxford, the Bulldogs rallied to defeat Florida in Jacksonville. Behind 27-13 at halftime, the Dogs scored on their second possession of the second half to pull within 27-20. Then the Gators moved deep into Bulldog territory and gambled on a fourth-down play, which became known as "Fourth and Dumb." Johnny Henderson anticipated the play and threw the Gators' Earl Carr for a loss.

Goff and the Bulldogs churned out yardage at will, and the Gators never threatened again, with the Bulldogs wining 41-27.

There was a close call versus Georgia Tech in Athens, but Allan Leavitt's late field goal decided the game. The Bulldogs won the SEC title for the first time in seven years, and Vince Dooley's third championship.

"Yeah, Yeah, Yeah!"

Oct. 28, 1978 · Georgia 17, Kentucky 16

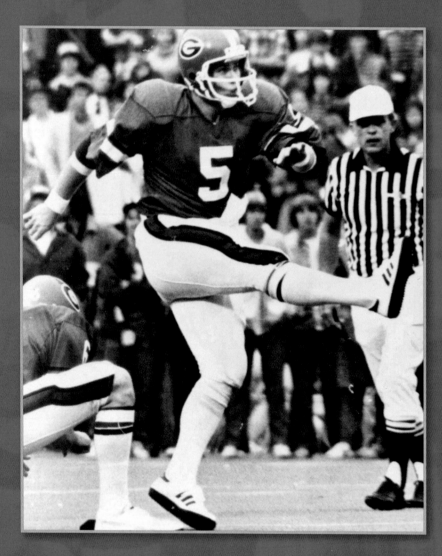

(Left) Rex Robinson kicks the game-winning field goal against Kentucky in 1978. (Opposite page) Quarterback Jeff Pyburn follows his blockers against the Wildcats.

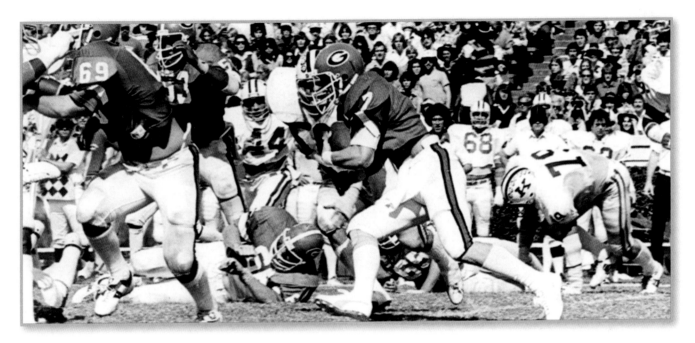

As the 1970s came to a close, it appeared the pattern with the Georgia football team was that it took a bad year to bring about a good year.

In 1977, little went right for the Bulldogs, who finished 5-6, Vince Dooley's only losing season. The circumstance was exacerbated by the up-and-down pattern of the '70s. If the offense was productive, the defense was lacking, and vice versa.

The Bulldogs needed a banner year when the season opened in 1978 with the 16-14 defeat of Baylor on Sept. 16. Cautious optimism caused excitement, as the Bulldogs won eight of nine games, losing only to South Carolina in Columbia, a non-conference game at the time. Georgia's 12-0 defeat of Clemson was the Tigers' only loss of the season.

At Auburn, the Bulldogs rallied three times to move in position to win a game that would have given them the SEC title. Midway through the final period, Georgia drove 63 yards to score when Willie McClendon dove over from the 1 and Rex Robinson kicked the conversion with 5:18 remaining. After the game, Dooley apologized to the team for not going for two points after the last touchdown. With that much time, he was making a percentage decision, but it made his team feel better about the tie when he

announced to them that he had made a coaching mistake.

One of the most memorable road victories came against Kentucky in Lexington, when Robinson kicked the winning field goal. Down 16-0 midway through the third quarter, the Bulldogs rallied to score two touchdowns, led by quarterback Jeff Pyburn. With 4:03 left, Pyburn guided the Dogs down to the Kentucky 12, when Robinson went in for a field-goal attempt.

Kentucky tried to "ice" Robinson by calling time-out twice, but when his kick sailed through, Georgia announcer Larry Munson, whose popularity and legend was passionately building, never said the kick was good, but instead screamed into the microphone, "Yeah, yeah, yeah!"

That turned out to be one of Munson's greatest calls, other classics notwithstanding. It was a crisp, cool night in Lexington, and WSB's Clear Channel signal penetrated the airwaves into the Midwest, probably all the way to Minnesota, where Munson was born. Munson would be toasted across many borders after that broadcast. Thousands heard the call, many of whom had no vested interest in the game. They became Georgia fans that night and, without question, Larry Munson fans.

SCAN TO WATCH

FOOTAGE FROM

THE VICTORY

BUCK TO AMP BEATS TECH

Dec. 2, 1978 · Georgia 29, Georgia Tech 28

(Above) Freshman quarterback Buck Belue
ran and passed the Bulldogs to victory over
Georgia Tech.

You could count on Georgia's 1978 team to win the close games, the 22-22 tie with Auburn being the only exception. The Kentucky game had Bulldog hearts thumping — conference game on the road, harvest season, an autumn night and an unforgettable comeback.

Against Georgia Tech, fumbles and penalties plagued the Bulldogs early on. Tech jumped out to a 20-0 lead, including the recovery of an onside kick that led to a score. The Bulldogs had to stop the bleeding. Suddenly, Tech's offense became docile while Georgia began slowly fashioning a spectacular comeback.

Freshman quarterback Buck Belue, now the full-time signal caller with Jeff Pyburn injured, directed a Bulldog drive of 55 yards to make the score 20-7 in favor of the visitors. In the third quarter, Scott Woerner intercepted a Jacket pass and returned it to the Tech 39 to set up the Bulldogs' second touchdown. A few plays later, Woerner went the distance with a Tech punt, 72 yards, and Georgia had the lead at 21-20. The advantage was short-lived, however, as Tech's Drew Hill returned the ensuing kickoff for 100 yards, followed by a two-point conversion.

With 5:52 left in the game and everybody on the edge of their seat, the Valdosta-born Belue went to work from his own 16-yard line and found the challenge stiff and foreboding. On fourth down, he scrambled to his right, which drew the Tech defense to the corner, thinking he had made the decision to run for a first down. Belue spotted Anthony "Amp" Arnold, an Athens boy, behind the Tech secondary, pulled up and fired a pass, straight and true. Arnold caught the ball and raced 46 yards for a touchdown. Sanford Stadium turned upside down, but there was still work to be done.

It was no surprise that the Bulldogs opted for the two-point conversion. After an interference call on an incomplete pass, receivers coach Charley Whittemore signaled for Arnold, lined up at flanker, to get the ball coming around end and taking a pitch

from Belue. Tech closed hard and almost got to Belue, but he pitched flawlessly to the speeding Arnold, who raced to the corner untouched.

Later in a conversation with Arnold about his touchdown catch, he explained the play. "When I saw the defense close on Buck, I waved my arms, and he saw me. When the pass got to me, I was wide open. All I had to do was catch it and cruise."

(Above) Anthony "Amp" Arnold scored the final touchdown and two-point conversion to beat the Yellow Jackets.

SCAN TO WATCH WALKER'S FIRST TOUCHDOWN

HERSCHEL EXPLODES ONTO THE SCENE

Sept. 6, 1980 · Georgia 16, Tennessee 15

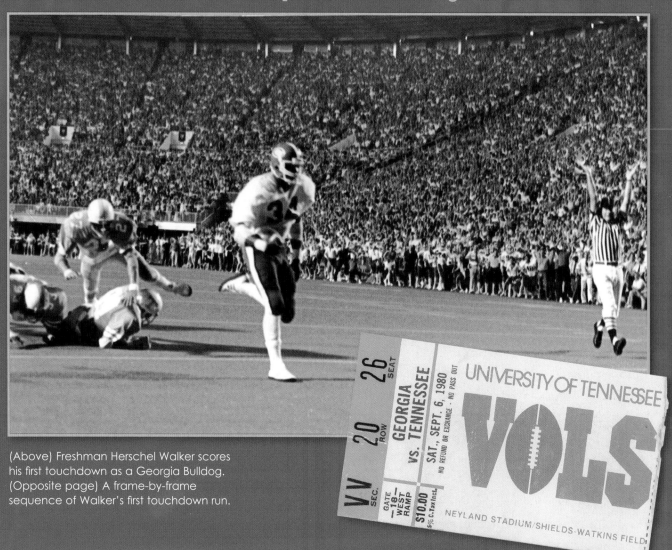

(Above) Freshman Herschel Walker scores his first touchdown as a Georgia Bulldog. (Opposite page) A frame-by-frame sequence of Walker's first touchdown run.

UNIVERSITY OF TENNESSEE

VOLS

GEORGIA VS. TENNESSEE
SAT., SEPT. 6, 1980
NO REFUND OR EXCHANGE · NO PASS OUT

SEC. VV
GATE —18—
WEST
RAMP
ROW 20
SEAT 26
$10.00
5% C.TaxIncl.

NEYLAND STADIUM/SHIELDS-WATKINS FIELD

The opening game with Tennessee in 1980 had as much to do with musings about Herschel Walker — "How will this Class-A running back, less than four months removed from his senior prom, fare in the hard-nosed Southeastern Conference?" — as it did about the matchup with a fine Volunteer team, one that UT coach Johnny Majors thought had exceptional championship potential.

It was a night game, hot and sticky, with 95,288 fans crammed into their seats. The first half, Georgia could not gain any momentum offensively. Donnie McMickens (long the subject of Bulldog trivia) started the game at tailback. Herschel did not make an appearance until the second quarter. Hidden in the accounts of the game is a play he made that was nearly as consequential as his two touchdown runs, when he recovered Buck Belue's fumble at the Georgia 31-yard line, an effort that reflected his competitive instincts and his remarkable speed. The Georgia coaches marveled at that play as much as they did his running skills, which would be displayed during the second half.

A safety — Belue fumbled at the Georgia 1 and Jimmy Wommack recovered in the end zone — and a touchdown gave the home team a 9-0 advantage at the half. A touchdown followed by a failed two-point conversion attempt added another six points to Tennessee's total.

While Herschel rightly gets credit for sparking the Bulldogs to victory, it should not go unnoticed that there were multiple heroes that night, which are required to win big games. When center Joe Happe — playing special teams only because of a padded cast on a broken right hand — the ball and Tennessee's Bill Bates converged at the same time, on a punt Georgia got its first break. The dropped ball was chased through the end zone for a safety. Finally, the scoreboard reflected points for the visitors, but Tennessee led 15-2.

Near the conclusion of the third quarter, Herschel, confident and savvy, ran through the Tennessee defense 16 yards for a touchdown. Tennessee led 15-9, but from the Georgia vantage point, victory was in reach. Herschel scored again early in the fourth quarter, and the Bulldogs went out front 16-15, which became the final score.

However, it took several big plays to ensure victory. Pat McShea recovered a fumble, caused by Nate Taylor, at the Georgia 1-yard line to stop what could have been the winning drive for Tennessee. Then, a career punt of 47 yards by Jim Broadway allowed for favorable field position as the Bulldogs tried to keep the Vols out of field-goal range. The Georgia defense tightened and time ran out.

The story of the game was Herschel Walker, "the kid out of Wrightsville." But, in truth, he was no kid.

"RUN, LINDSAY, RUN"

Nov. 8, 1980 · Georgia 26, Florida 21

To win a championship, a team must win close games. Few national championship teams won more close games than Georgia in 1980.

It began with the comeback win in Knoxville in the opener. Then there was the Clemson game in Sanford Stadium when Scott Woerner retuned a punt for a touchdown and also returned an intercepted pass 98 yards to the Clemson 2-yard line, where quarterback Buck Belue sneaked across to give the Bulldogs a 14-0 lead. Clemson, ambitious and tenacious, fought back with 10 points in the second quarter and two field goals in the second half, while Georgia's Rex Robinson added a pair of field goals to make the final score 20-16.

Then South Carolina — with its vaunted back George Rogers, who would win the Heisman Trophy — came to play between the hedges. Herschel Walker outplayed Rogers, and many thought he should have earned the Heisman, but who is going to vote for a freshman? Herschel had a brilliant 76-yard touchdown run and Robinson added two field goals for a 13-10 victory, but it was the defense that saved the day when Bulldogs Dale Carver and Woerner forced Rogers to fumble, with Tim Parks recovering the loose ball.

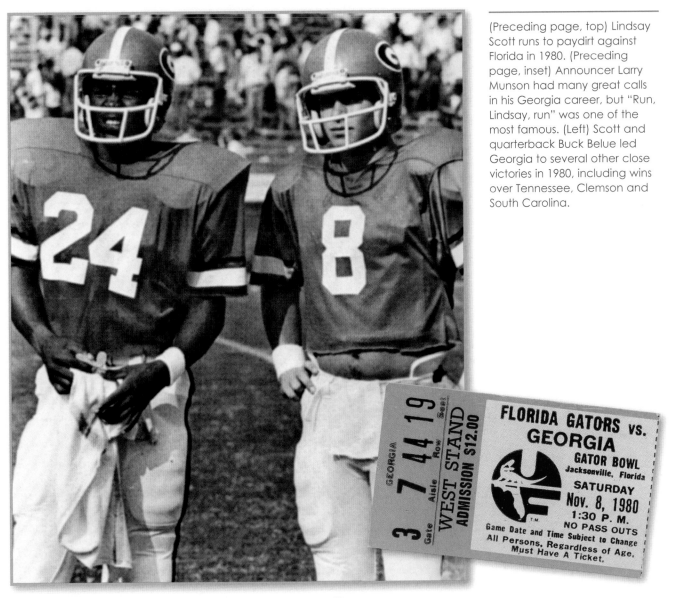

(Preceding page, top) Lindsay Scott runs to paydirt against Florida in 1980. (Preceding page, inset) Announcer Larry Munson had many great calls in his Georgia career, but "Run, Lindsay, run" was one of the most famous. (Left) Scott and quarterback Buck Belue led Georgia to several other close victories in 1980, including wins over Tennessee, Clemson and South Carolina.

The Bulldogs had left everything on the field in the South Carolina game and were not crisp and sharp for the matchup with Florida in the old Gator Bowl. They lacked that performance edge, but not by much. Georgia led 14-10 at the half and 20-10 at the end of the third quarter, but Florida kept chipping away, finally taking a 21-20 lead on a field goal with 6:52 left in the game.

When Georgia took over at its own 7-yard line with a minute and a half left, Florida fans began to celebrate. After a couple of incomplete passes, the Bulldogs had not given up. A first down and then another and a couple more — move the chains — and Robinson could kick the game winner.

Suddenly, lightening struck. Belue, rolling to his right and getting a key block from Nat Hudson — who peeled off a block at the line of scrimmage to knock a blitzing linebacker out of the way — saw roommate Lindsay Scott open over the middle. Buck fired high over the heads of the defense but just right for Scott, who jumped up for the ball, caught it, came down and tucked it. He ran toward the Georgia sideline, getting to the corner. It was now a footrace, and Scott would not be denied. "Run, Lindsay, run," Larry Munson pleaded on the air. Touchdown!

The miracle was consummated: Georgia 26, Florida 21.

(Preceding page) Herschel Walker in the open field against Florida. (Above) Belue, center, talks things over with a couple of teammates in 1980. (Right) Belue and Scott embrace after the game-winning touchdown over the Gators.

A NATIONAL CHAMPIONSHIP
Jan. 1, 1981 · Georgia 17, Notre Dame 10

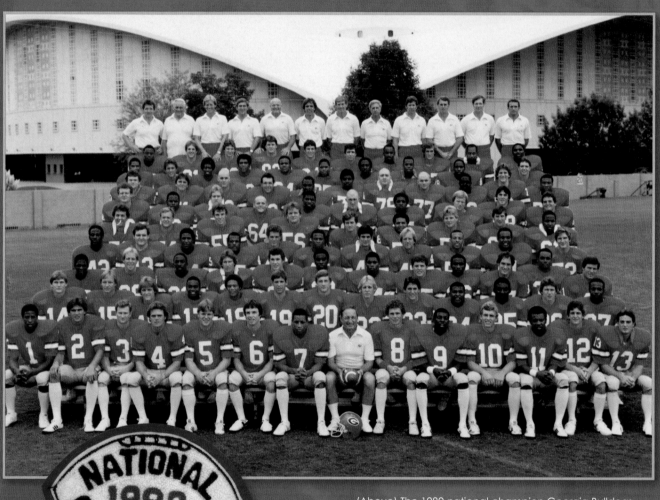

(Above) The 1980 national champion Georgia Bulldogs.

As Georgia celebrated victory in the aftermath of the Florida game, a funny thing was taking place on Grant Field in Atlanta, where Georgia Tech — a team that would finish with a 1-9-1 record — tied Notre Dame, which was unbeaten and ranked No. 1.

That enabled the Bulldogs to travel to Auburn the next week as the nation's top-ranked team. Georgia would defeat Auburn 31-21, and Georgia Tech in the last game of the season, 38-20, as Herschel Walker finished with 1,616 yards rushing, the most ever by a freshman running back.

Bulldog partisans flocked to New Orleans for the national championship game, forming the "red sea" in the French Quarter. Keith Jackson, a native of Roopville in Carroll County, would call the game for ABC-TV. Vernon Brinson, a Bulldog baseball letterman in the early 1960s, would host the Georgia team at Sugar Bowl functions, as every Bulldog from Hahira to Blairsville to Tybee Light scrambled for a ticket to the game.

The centerpiece of the Crescent City experience was, of course, the game — and what a game it was. It was another close one, with the Bulldogs finding a way "one more time," as defensive coordinator Erskine Russell preached. The final score in the Louisiana Superdome was 17-10. Highlights of the game included: two touchdowns by Herschel Walker; a blocked field goal by freshman Terry Hoage; brothers Bob and Steve Kelly recovering a kickoff that went "unfielded" by the Irish, which the Bulldogs later claimed was the longest onside kick recovery in history of college football; two interceptions by Scott Woerner, one in the closing minute of play to seal victory, with Notre Dame driving for a tying score.

But the story of the game was Walker — not the two touchdowns he scored, and not the 150 yards he gained against Notre Dame's defense, which vowed

(Right) Herschel Walker takes a breather on the bench during the national championship game in New Orleans.

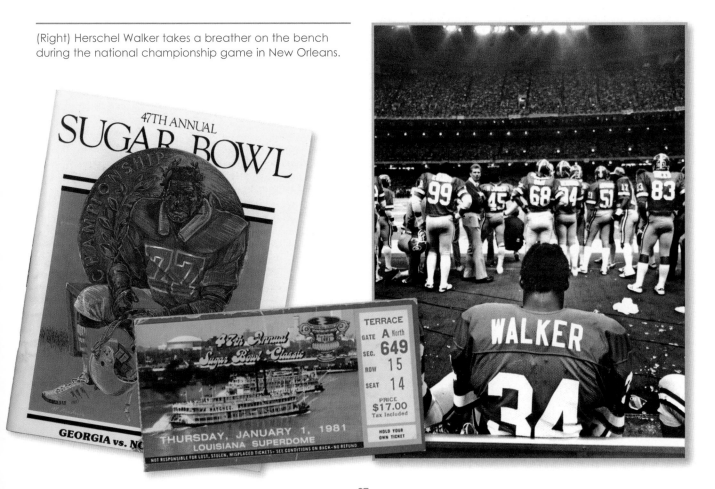

87

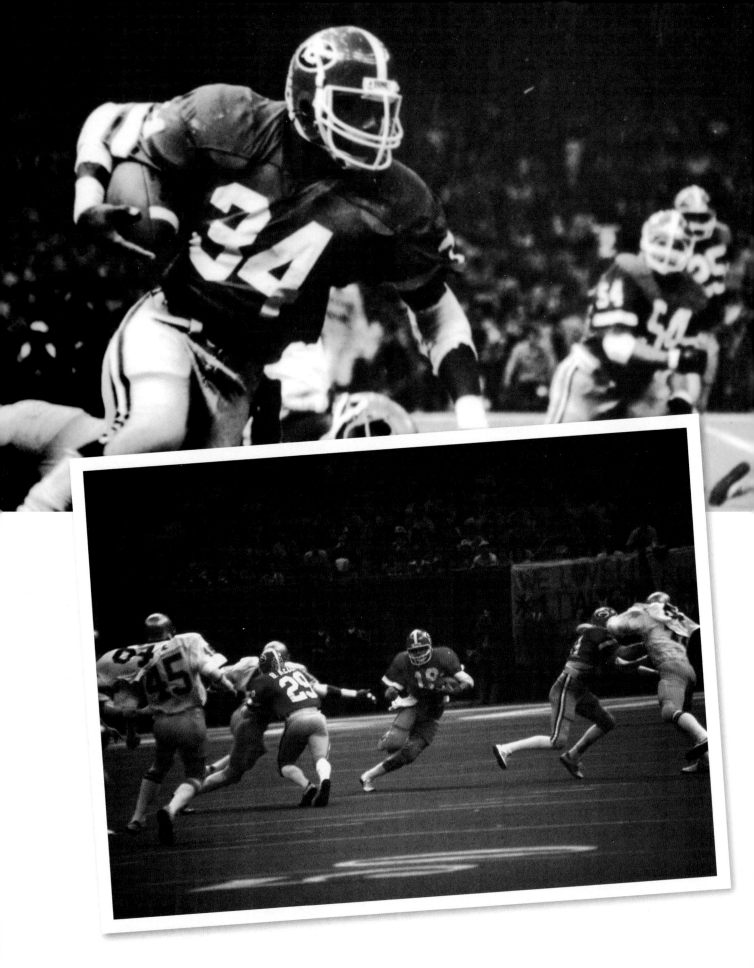

pre-game to hold him to less than 100 yards rushing. But the story was that Walker played the game with a dislocated shoulder!

It happened on the first offensive series. When Herschel came to the sideline and met with trainer Warren Morris and Dr. Butch Mulherin, they were pale-faced. Vince Dooley, upon hearing the news, thought, "Whatever we do today, we'll have to do it without Herschel."

Herschel grimaced, said nothing, and returned to the game the next offensive series. You, like all Georgia fans, know the rest of the story. He ignored the pain and took 34 snaps to lead his team to victory.

Later, Bulldog fans, on an unparalleled high, danced in the streets, some chanting "Three More Years!" That would, of course, be Herschel's remaining years of eligibility.

(Preceding page, top) Walker ran for 150 yards and two touchdowns against Notre Dame, and he did it with a dislocated shoulder. (Preceding page, bottom) Scott Woerner intercepted two passes in the Sugar Bowl Classic. (Above) Gov. George Busbee and coach Vince Dooley pose for a photo before the flight to New Orleans.

SCAN TO HEAR   LARRY MUNSON'S   CALL

"SUGAR FALLING OUT OF THE SKY"

Nov. 13, 1982 · Georgia 19, Auburn 14

(Above) The Georgia-Auburn game is always close and intense. (Opposite page) Quarterback John Lastinger throws while on the run against Auburn.

At Auburn in 1982, the home team was focused keenly on bringing about the first defeat of the season for the Georgia Bulldogs, who were again in the hunt for a national title.

In 1981, only Clemson had been able to defeat the defending national champions in the regular season. For a three-year stretch, with Herschel Walker giving every linebacker in the league a headache, Georgia would not lose a conference game.

The Georgia-Auburn game is always close and intense, and has been since the first time the two teams met in February 1892. While Auburn was twice beaten in 1892, 90 years later, the Tigers were at home and they were primed for an upset.

Even with Georgia's offensive firepower, it was the defense that saved the day this time. This was the memorable game when Auburn's fourth-down pass was broken up with 49 seconds left to play, and Larry Munson excited the Bulldog Nation, as he so often

did: "Oh, look at the sugar falling out of the sky." While the Red and Black patrons celebrated, at least one inebriated Auburn fan took exception. He walked into the Georgia radio booth and splashed his drink into Munson's face. Munson casually noted, "Somebody threw something on us."

To relive the moment, you refer to the play-by-play and note that Georgia had its back to the wall after Lionel James ran 87 yards from scrimmage to put Auburn ahead 14-13 with 13:54 remaining on the clock.

John Lastinger, the one-time Bulldog receiver now playing quarterback, then directed a drive of 80 yards. He gave the ball to Herschel — who gained 177 yards on the afternoon — eight times on the drive, and mixed in timely passes to give the lead back to Georgia, 19-14, when Herschel scored from 3 yards out.

There was time left for Auburn, as Munson said,

"to break our hearts." The Tigers responded from their own 20 and had everybody on their feet. Auburn converted three third-down plays and suddenly had a first down at the Georgia 11-yard line with 2:39 remaining. On first down, Bo Jackson was thrown for a 2-yard loss. On the next snap, Dale Carver threw Auburn quarterback Randy Campbell for another loss, making it third and 26. Campbell completed a pass for 9 yards, and on fourth down, looked for a receiver in the Georgia end zone, when

safety Jeff Sanchez and cornerback Ronnie Harris broke up the pass and broke Auburn's hearts.

The victory ensured the top-ranked Bulldogs would be playing in the Sugar Bowl against Penn State.

(Above) Lastinger started out as a receiver at Georgia. (Opposite page) The Georgia defense brings down Auburn quarterback Randy Campbell.

HERSCHEL WINS THE HEISMAN

1982

(Left) Herschel Walker with his 1982 Heisman Trophy. (Opposite page) Walker's jersey and helmet are on display in the Butts-Mehre Building on the UGA campus.

The Herschel Walker years were memorable ones. Three Southeastern Conference titles and a national championship. Three times he made All-America and won the Heisman Trophy in 1982. Perhaps he should have won another Heisman.

There was a bittersweet ending to his career. All of Athens was crestfallen when Herschel turned pro in the winter of 1983. Those of us who know him believed, deep down, he really did not want to leave. But he played with fire and got burned when the upstart USFL's New Jersey Generals essentially said,

"Here, sign this contract and sleep on it and we'll understand if you change your mind in the morning." Herschel believed that to be in good faith, walked the campus all night and was ready to politely tell the Generals he was remaining in school for his senior year. Too late. Team officials had made copies of the contract. When Vince Dooley learned of the contract and saw a copy, he had no choice but to declare Herschel, by NCAA rules, ineligible.

When things settled and Herschel had moved on, all Georgia men and women who were downcast with the circumstances had to express their disap-

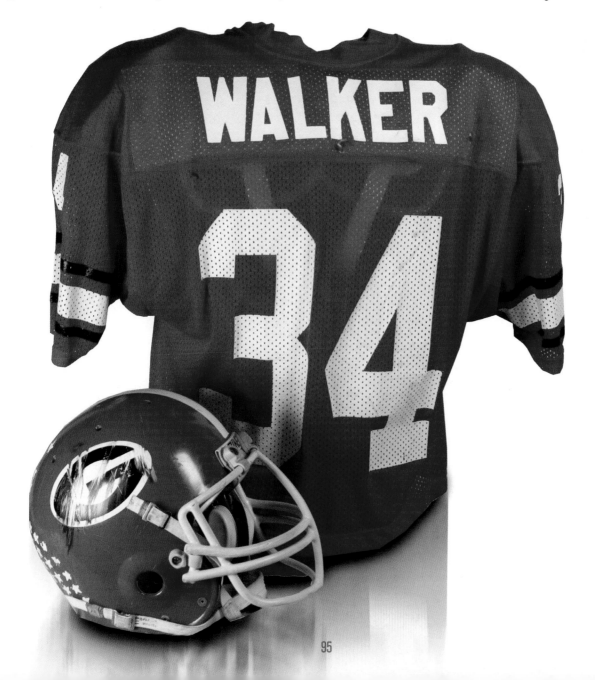

pointment with a heart-warming caveat. We hated to see him go, but raised a toast to the fact that he had come our way.

In December 1982, Herschel boarded a Delta flight to New York with coach Dooley, Claude Felton and a couple other folks, heading to the Big Apple for the Heisman announcement. Herschel should have won the Heisman his freshman year, as the statistics show that, and he might have won if the vote had been taken at the end of the season and not following the 10th game against Auburn. In 1981, Marcus Allen, the winner, had a remarkable year with 2,342 rushing yards, while Herschel gained 1,891. Herschel finished third and second before winning the trophy in 1982. Assuming he had stayed for his senior year and had posted yardage totals as he had done in the three previous years, you would think he probably would have won a second Heisman.

At the Downtown Athletic Club, deep on the southern tip of Manhattan, there was a tense atmosphere in the room, as sportscaster Dick Schaap readied himself for the announcement and an opportunity to interview the winner.

John Elway (Stanford), Eric Dickerson (SMU), Anthony Carter (Michigan) and Dave Rimington (Nebraska) were huddled with Herschel when the announcement came that the winner wore the Red and Black of the Bulldogs.

Glory, Glory to Old Georgia!

(Below) Walker's last of three All-America certificates he earned at UGA. (Opposite page) In March 1982, *Sports Illustrated* was about nine months premature on speculating that Walker would turn professional.

Sports Illustrated

MARCH 1, 1982 $1.50

WILL HERSCHEL WALKER TURN PRO NOW?

A COTTON BOWL VICTORY

Jan. 1, 1984 · Georgia 10, Texas 9

(Above) Quarterback John Lastinger celebrates scoring the game-winning touchdown against second-ranked Texas in the 1984 Cotton Bowl.

All good things do come to an end, and so it was after Herschel Walker joined the New Jersey Generals. Georgia began the 1983 season without an established running back. Good recruits had shunned the Bulldogs, not wanting to ride the bench with Herschel in the backfield.

The bottom didn't fall out, however, and the Bulldogs came close to winning a fourth straight SEC title without Herschel, finishing 10-1-1 and receiving invitation to the Cotton Bowl to play No. 2 Texas.

A 16-16 tie at Clemson was a disappointment, but the Bulldogs were undefeated when they got to Jacksonville, where they were heavy underdogs against Florida. They found a way to win, 10-9, on a 16-play, 99-yard drive. The score would be symbolic after the comeback Cotton Bowl victory over Texas.

Auburn, behind Bo Jackson, eked out a hard-fought 13-7 win in Sanford Stadium the next week, and Georgia's dominance in the SEC was over. The disappointed Dawgs defeated Georgia Tech 27-25 in Atlanta, as Tony Flack intercepted a John Dewberry pass in the closing minute of play to seal the victory.

The Cotton Bowl didn't produce any fireworks until the end of the game. It was a defensive struggle from the start, both defenses refusing to allow a touchdown. Field goals were the best the Longhorns and Bulldogs could muster for three quarters, with Texas making three and Georgia one.

On the Georgia sideline late in the final quarter, Vince Dooley, a patient and fundamentals-oriented coach, watched his team routinely punt in the closing minutes of play. But the punt slipped through the arms of the Texas punt returner, and Gary Moss recovered for Georgia at the Horns' 23-yard line. The Dawgs had new life.

As it had been most of the afternoon, the Bulldogs could not find a crack in the Longhorn defense, moving the ball 6 yards in two running plays. Dooley said to offensive coordinator George Haffner on the phone, "George you gotta put it up." Haffner's sug-

gestion was to run John Lastinger on the option. Dooley acquiesced, a storyline many Dooley Ball second-guessers might find difficult to believe.

Lastinger took the snap, moved to his right, and suddenly found a hole off tackle. He raced through and sprinted to the corner, hitting the pylon and ending up in a heap at the goal line, with Texas defenders all converging at the same time. He was not sure he had scored until he looked up at the official's upraised arms.

With that, Lastinger said out loud, "Glory to Ole Georgia."

(Above) Gary Moss gave the Bulldogs new life when he recovered a fumbled punt late in the game against the Longhorns.

THE BUTLER DID IT

Sept. 22, 1984 · Georgia 26, Clemson 23

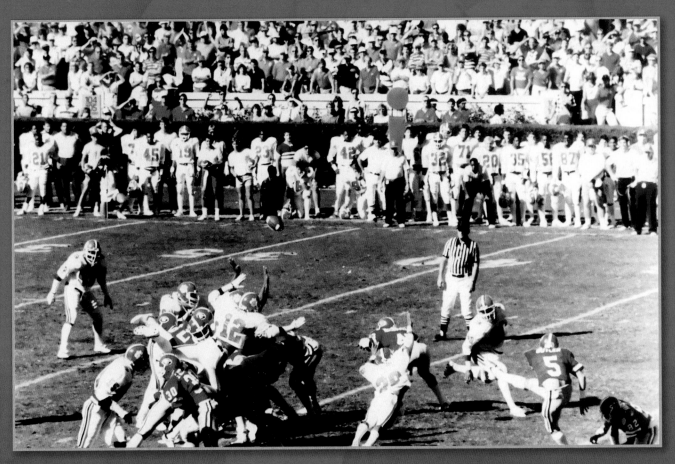

(Above) Kevin Butler kicks a 60-yard
field goal with just seconds remaining
in the game to beat Clemson in 1984.
Butler went on to have a prolific NFL
career with the Chicago Bears and
Arizona Cardinals.

The mid-1980s were not the best of times for Vince Dooley and the Bulldogs, though they were not the worst — certainly nothing like the up-and-down times of the '70s.

After the infamous Jan Kemp trial in which the athletic association was the victim of a lawsuit aimed at the university administration, President Dr. Fred Davison ordained that Georgia would take no partial qualifiers in recruiting. Yet Georgia had to line up against teams that had not just one, but several non-qualifiers.

Even with that internal decision, the Bulldogs fielded winning teams and received a bowl invitation every year. There were several highlights during this time, and in 1984, one of the biggest individual feats in the kicking game in Georgia history took place against Clemson in Sanford Stadium.

Georgia began playing Clemson in 1897 and holds a commanding 41-17-4 record in the series. In the John Heisman era at Clemson (1899-1904), the Tigers won five of six games. After that, the Bulldogs have dominated, losing only six times in 35 years.

The Dawgs had the premier kicker in college football in Kevin Butler. An outstanding high school player at Redan High in DeKalb County, Butler had injured his knee but was told by Dooley that he still had a scholarship at Georgia.

Butler became one of the most prolific kickers ever for the Bulldogs, setting records, his right foot often the difference in games throughout his career. Never was his deciding toe more dramatic than when his kick won the Clemson game between the hedges his senior year.

When Dooley sent Butler in to attempt a 60-yard field goal with seconds left on the clock, the stadium buzzed with uncommon excitement. They knew the yardage, and they knew they were watching history in the making if Butler's kick went through the uprights.

On the field, the Georgia players moved eagerly up to the sideline, positioning themselves to see But-ler's attempt. When Butler hit the ball, they knew his foot had made solid contact. As the kick arched high, they knew it had a chance. Suddenly, they began to cheer and jump up and down. They knew it was good. Butler held his breath, but he knew it was long enough. When the officials raised their arms upright in confirmation, pandemonium enveloped the stands. Not only was the kick good, but it won the game 26-23 with 11 seconds remaining on the clock.

(Above) Cleveland Gary scored on a 1-yard run late in the third quarter to tie the game at 20-20.

101

COACH DOOLEY'S

SCAN TO WATCH

LAST GAME

DOOLEY GOES OUT ON TOP

Jan. 1, 1989 · Georgia 34, Michigan State 27

(Left) Rodney Hampton turned in a huge performance in coach Vince Dooley's final game by rushing for 109 yards on 10 carries, catching four passes for 71 yards and scoring three touchdowns.

Every athlete, and every coach, wants to go out on top. In December 1989, Vince Dooley contemplated his future. Unbeknownst to his friends and associates, including University of Georgia colleagues and officials, he was thinking of retiring from the sideline.

His achievements were notable and of the highest realm. He had won a national championship, he had been named Coach of the Year by the American Football Coaches Association, he had been president of the AFCA, and he had won 200 games. He knew that when he was eligible, he would be a cinch for the College Football Hall of Fame.

His coaching career would end in the Gator Bowl in 1989. The Bulldogs would be playing a very capable Michigan State team, but the "Silver Seniors" — the name the seniors on the team gave themselves as the 25th Dooley class — were determined to send their coach into retirement with a victory. It would not be easy, however.

The Spartans, coached by George Perles — who had been a defensive coach and coordinator on the Pittsburgh Steelers' four Super Bowl teams — had an explosive offense led by talented receiver Andre Rison, who later played for the Atlanta Falcons and subsequently won a Super Bowl ring with the Green Bay Packers.

Dooley decided that it would be best to air it out if the Bulldogs were going to win his final game. He sat down with offensive coordinator George Haffner, who had aspirations to succeed Dooley, and said, "Throw it as often as you want to." The old Dawg was departing from convention.

Georgia led 17-7 at the half and 27-13 at the end of the third quarter. Rodney Hampton's 32-yard dash for a score with 11:58 remaining in the fourth quarter put the Bulldogs up 34-20. Then Rison scored on a 50-yard reception with 3:49 remaining, but after the ensuing kickoff, the Bulldogs controlled the clock to win a thriller and send Dooley into retirement with a 34-27 victory.

A new life awaited Dooley as he became Georgia's full-time athletic director. His vision and leadership would bode well for the overall Bulldog athletic program. Dooley also became a master gardener and gained a reputation as a landscaping expert. He found time to author several books, and you'll now find him traveling to speak here, exploring a historical site there — all the while maintaining a pace that younger men could not match.

Vince Dooley: a Damn Good Dawg!

(Below) Dooley rides off into the sunset on the shoulders of his players in the Gator Bowl. The College Football Hall of Famer's record was 201-77-10.

Bulldogs Show Tigers Their Teeth

Nov. 16, 1996 · Georgia 56, Auburn 49

(Above) Quarterback Mike Bobo rifles a pass against Auburn in 1996. (Right) Hines Ward caught a 67-yard touchdown pass from Bobo in the fourth quarter.

Georgia had two big reasons to celebrate its trip to Auburn in 1996. First, the Bulldogs dramatically defeated Auburn in the first overtime game in the Southeastern Conference — it was the 100th anniversary of the series — and Uga took offense at an Auburn receiver's taunt.

Down 28-7 in the second quarter, the Bulldogs, behind quarterback Mike Bobo, rallied for a touchdown with 37 seconds left in the period. Auburn then led 28-14 at the half.

Auburn would not score in the final two quarters, which is a reminder that for all the offensive heroics, the defense deserves a generous salute. While the defense shut out the Tigers in the second half, Bobo went to work on offense. He connected with Hines Ward early in the fourth quarter for a 67-yard touchdown, and Auburn's lead was reduced to seven points.

On the Bulldogs' final possession in the fourth quarter, Bobo managed the clock like a seasoned Johnny Unitas in his heyday with the Baltimore Colts. Bobo kept hitting receivers over the middle and then getting the next play off by the time the clock started again, working it to perfection. He hit Ward on a sideline route, and the Dawgs had the ball deep in Auburn territory.

Then Georgia hearts sank, as Bobo was sacked at the 30-yard line with three seconds left. Bobo spiked the ball, and one second remained when the offensive line gave their quarterback enough protection for him to fire a 30-yard touchdown pass to Corey Allen at the Auburn goal line for the tying touchdown.

In the fourth overtime period after each team had scored matching touchdowns to extend the overtime, Torin Kirtsey scored from 1 yard out. Auburn, on what turned out to be its last possession, could not get the ball into the end zone. It was time for a history-making celebration.

As sensational and stunning as the overtime victory was, the thing that Georgia fans seemed to enjoy the most came after Auburn scored its first touchdown on a pass reception by Robert Baker. As Baker came down with the ball and stepped into the end zone, his momentum carried him within arms' length of Georgia mascot Uga V. Uga took offense and leaped in Baker's direction, straining maddeningly at his leash, causing Charles Seiler to hang on for dear life.

Patricia Miklik, photographer for the *Montgomery Advertiser*, caught the action on her camera. The newspaper got so many requests for copies of the photo that the negative wore completely out. Today, a print of the photo remains a prized possession for many Georgia fans — Sonny Seiler included.

(Below) Torin Kirtsey scored what would be the game-winning touchdown in the fourth overtime against the Tigers. After the Bulldog defense stopped Auburn on its next possession, it was time for a history-making celebration.

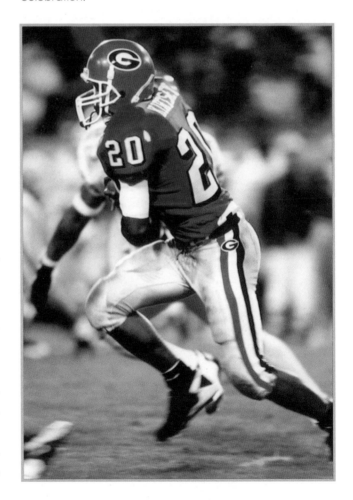

EDWARDS, DEFENSE TOP GATORS

Nov. 1, 1997 · Georgia 37, Florida 17

(Left) Robert Edwards goes airborne for one of his four touchdowns against Florida in 1997. (Above) Orantes Grant brings down a Gator. The defense came up big against UF, with relentless pressure and four interceptions, including two by Kirby Smart.

Historically in the Georgia-Florida series, the Bulldogs had the advantage, but that changed when Vince Dooley retired and Steve Spurrier became the Gator coach.

At this point in the rivalry, the schedule changed. Traditionally, Florida played Auburn the week before the big game in Jacksonville, while Georgia usually scheduled a weaker non-conference opponent. Playing tough games back to back for Florida in that situation gave the Bulldogs an advantage. Spurrier realized that and influenced a schedule change to where, in many years, Florida had an open date before the Georgia game in Jacksonville. Then the rotation of the schedule, dictated by the Southeastern Conference, often caused Georgia to wind up in the position of playing two big rival games, namely Arkansas and LSU, back to back. For years, Kentucky was in that pre-Florida slot, and while Georgia has historically had the advantage in the series with the Wildcats, it remained a conference game. It is not easy to travel to Lexington and then immediately to Jacksonville and get your team ready for a rivalry game.

In 1990, Georgia had a 44-22-2 record in the series, but the Bulldogs went into a swoon after that, with Florida dominating the series as the Bulldogs had in the early years. In 1997, however, Georgia dominated the game, with Robert Edwards scoring four touchdowns and the defense coming up with four interceptions. Florida was ranked No. 6 in the nation, and Georgia's victory was no fluke.

It was Robert Edwards Day, but it could have also been Hines Ward Day, as the multifaceted Bulldog star accounted for 203 total yards. Let's also hear it for Mike Bobo, the quarterback who completed 16 of 27 passes for 260 yards, as his performance was noteworthy as well. And those pass interceptions — two by Kirby Smart — were timely. All day long, the defense rushed the Florida passer with limitless passion. They would not be denied.

Edwards, who grew up in Sandersville, an hour

and a half south of Athens, came to Georgia with a fine football reputation. He first lined up on defense, where he excelled because he was a competitive, gifted athlete. Friends in Washington County used to ask, "Why don't you put Robert Edwards on offense? He is the best running back we ever had here." When Edwards moved over to offense, he became one of the most prolific running backs at Georgia since Herschel Walker and Garrison Hearst.

The win over Florida in Jacksonville was a good tonic for the Georgia faithful, who had not experienced a celebration in eight long years.

(Below) Hines Ward accounted for 203 total yards against the Gators.

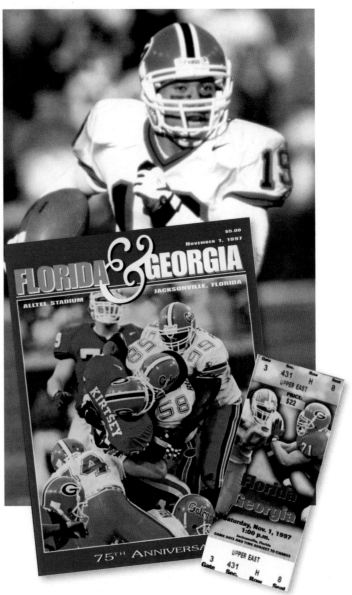

RICHT TAKES OVER THE BULLDOGS

Dec. 26, 2000

(Above) Georgia Athletic Director Vince Dooley introduces new head coach Mark Richt on Dec. 26, 2000. Within two years, Richt had the Bulldogs back in the SEC Championship Game.

ark Richt was named head coach of the Bulldogs on Dec. 26, 2000. He arrived in Athens from Florida State with a perceptive knowledge of the Georgia program. Tallahassee is less than an hour from Thomasville, and Richt had for years observed what was going on at Georgia. He recruited the state and noticed the passion of the Bulldog fans in Thomasville, where the FSU team headquartered on Friday nights before home games.

Richt's mother, Helen, remembers that as his reputation as Bobby Bowden's offensive coordinator began to be noticed, regionally and nationally, that in conversations with her son about becoming a head coach, "He always said that if the Georgia job came open he would be very interested," she said. "He always believed that the Bulldog job had to be one of the best in the country."

One day, he and I were riding through the campus in the springtime, on the way to the airport for a meeting somewhere. He was visibly taken by the beauty of the campus and the energy of the students as they were making their way to class. He was focused intently on the campus scene, and without any prompting, exclaimed with an enthusiastic smile, "To mess this thing up, you would almost have to try."

Georgia, when Richt was hired, had gone through two coaches and a long drought when it came to competing for the SEC championship. By the time Richt arrived on the scene, the conference had expanded to 12 teams with two divisions and an annual playoff for the championship at the Georgia Dome. It took Richt two years to win the right to play for the SEC title, and he did with a quarterback, David Greene, who was born on the Saturday in 1982 when Herschel Walker led Georgia to another victory over Florida.

Getting to the Dome in 2002 and defeating Arkansas for the championship was a moving experience for the Georgia alumni. They take pride in the fact that he has taken three other teams to Atlanta, with the 2005 winning of the conference title again. But like all fans, impatience prevails. They want to return to the Georgia Dome more often and they want to compete for a national championship. In case anybody is unaware, Mark Richt does, too.

In the meantime, remember what Richt stands for: Honesty, decency and forever trying to help his players find their way in life. As a Georgia graduate, I take pride in the fact that he wants to win the right way and that he will never embarrass the University of Georgia.

LARRY MUNSON'S
SCAN TO HEAR
FAMOUS CALL

THE HOBNAIL BOOT GAME
Oct. 6, 2001 · Georgia 26, Tennessee 24

(Above) Verron Haynes caught a 6-yard pass
from quarterback David Greene for the game-
winning touchdown against Tennessee.

Prior to Mark Richt's arrival at Georgia, bragging rights in the Tennessee series belonged to the Volunteers, who won nine straight games from 1989 through 1999 (the two teams did not play each other in 1990 and '91). In 2000, Jim Donnan's last Georgia team defeated Tennessee 21-10, as the students stormed the field and tore down the goal posts.

When Richt made his first trip to Knoxville in 2001, few would have bet on the underdog Bulldogs, but the new Georgia coach came up with a memorable victory in that first outing in Neyland Stadium.

David Greene, a redshirt freshman, had become the precocious starting quarterback and was leading the team like a seasoned veteran. Tennessee moved out front swiftly, 14-3, and some orange-clad Vol fans yawned, fully expecting the Bulldogs to succumb, as they had often done in the past.

In the second quarter, the scoring was reversed, with Georgia scoring 14 points and Tennessee three, and it was 17-17 at the half. There was no scoring in the third quarter, but Georgia took the lead with Billy Bennett's second field goal at 20-17 with 5:44 left in the game. Tennessee was bent on scoring a touchdown and eating up the clock against the upstart Bulldogs.

In the last minute of play, a Vol screen pass from Casey Clausen to Travis Stephens was good for a 62-yard touchdown. Several missed tackles had Georgia defensive coordinator Brian VanGorder fuming. The clock reflected 44 seconds remained. Jubilant Tennessee fans headed for the parking lots, convinced that the game was over, and many disappointed Bulldog fans followed.

The Richt-coached Bulldogs, especially the talented Greene, believed there was enough time to score. The Bulldogs practiced the two-minute drill every day at Woodruff Field, but they didn't have a 44-second plan.

Undaunted, they drove downfield from the Georgia 41-yard line. The sequence of plays follows:

- Freedom Top: Greene hit Damien Gary on an option route for a first down. The sideline was anxious, realizing that clock management could get the job done;

- Smoke: Incomplete pass to the wide receiver;

- 560 Switch: Pass completion over the middle to Randy McMichael for 26 yards;

- 44 Demon: Inside post to McMichael for 14 yards to 6-yard line.

This set up the play known as P-44 Haynes — Greene to Verron Haynes and a 26-24 victory.

Up in the radio booth, Larry Munson described the call, saying, "We just stepped on their face with a hobnail boot and broke their nose."

(Above) Greene, a redshirt freshman, led the Bulldogs like a seasoned veteran. With 44 seconds remaining from the Georgia 41-yard line, he engineered the winning drive in the 26-24 victory.

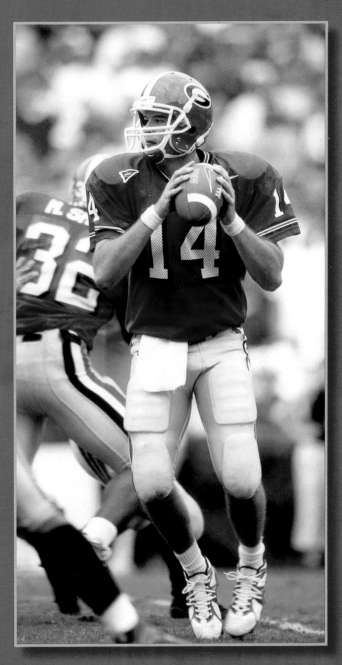

Dogs Rally To Beat Auburn

Nov. 16, 2002
Georgia 24, Auburn 21

When Georgia Tech exited the South-eastern Conference prior to the 1964 season, Georgia's last conference game became the Auburn game, which means that to win the SEC championship, the Bulldogs had to beat the Tigers for that honor. Later, defeating Auburn would often mean the Bulldogs were Eastern Division Champions with the right to play for the SEC title in the Georgia Dome.

Vince Dooley had to beat his old team six times to win the SEC title, and Mark Richt has had to do the same thing to get to the Georgia Dome. Four times, Richt's Georgia teams have downed the Tigers to win the SEC East and play for the championship. Beating Auburn has become more important than ever.

In 2002, the Bulldogs had championship on their minds when they journeyed over to the Plains with a 9-1 record. Even though the Dawgs had lost a heart-breaker to Florida, a win at Auburn would secure the SEC East crown.

Auburn led 14-3 at the half, which prompted a fiery halftime speech from tackle Jon Stinchcomb, who told his teammates they had worked too hard to get to this point and not accomplish their goals.

The Bulldogs scored 14 points in the third quarter, but Auburn scored a touchdown and led 21-17. On the second Bulldog score, you began to think that it might be Georgia's night, when David Greene called for a quarterback sneak at the Auburn goal line. He fumbled, but no harm done. Stinchcomb, his roommate, fell on the ball for a touchdown with 2:02 left in the quarter.

As time was running out in the fourth quarter, Greene, facing a second-and-6 situation at the Geor-gia 45-yard line, found receiver Fred Gibson open for a 41-yard gain that gave the Bulldogs much needed yardage and momentum. Following Gibson's catch at the Auburn 14, the Bulldogs needed a first down but soon found themselves facing a fourth-and-19 challenge following a false-start penalty. Seldom has a game been more on the line when Greene faded back and threw a pass with the perfect loft to enable Michael Johnson to outleap the Auburn defensive back and gather in the pass for a touch-down. The Bulldogs were a 24-21 victor and would play Arkansas in the Georgia Dome.

When you raise a toast to David and Michael, don't forget about the Georgia defense, led by Sean Jones, who had two interceptions and a fumble recovery. He also returned four punts for 75 yards.

Jones' play confirmed the time-honored notion that it takes a team effort to win big games. That was never more obvious than in Auburn on Nov. 16, 2002.

(Preceding page) On fourth and 19, David Greene faded back and threw a pass to Michael Johnson for a touchdown and a trip to the Georgia Dome. (Right) With Auburn leading 14-3, tackle Jon Stinchcomb delivered a fiery halftime speech, telling his teammates they had worked too hard to get to this point and not accomplish their goals.

AN SEC TITLE IN THE DOME

Dec. 7, 2002 · Georgia 30, Arkansas 3

(Above) David Pollack celebrates Georgia's 2002 SEC Championship with a sign from the Georgia Dome.

Georgia fans, especially those in metropolitan Atlanta, have had plenty of opportunities to visit the Georgia Dome for anything from Atlanta Falcons football to regional and national basketball events to concerts.

Mark Richt's 2002 team gave fans their first opportunity to visit the Dome to see the Bulldogs play in the SEC Championship Game.

Early on, you could sense that the Bulldogs had come to the Dome ready to take care of business. On the first punt of the game, Georgia's Decory Bryant came flying off the corner to block the Razorbacks' kick. Burt Jones, the special teams captain who had grown up watching Bulldog games with his parents and had walked on to play for Georgia, recovered the ball at the Arkansas 2-yard line. Jones and the punt block team had done their job, and the Bulldogs took a 7-0 lead when Musa Smith crossed the goal line while the jubilant Georgia stands celebrated.

That touchdown, as it turned out, would have been enough to win the game. All Arkansas could produce offensively was a field goal, as the Bulldogs won 30-3.

In the first quarter Georgia got out front 17-0 and added two Billy Bennett field goals in the second quarter for a 23-0 halftime lead. In the fourth quarter, David Greene and tight end Ben Watson connected for a 20-yard scoring pass with 12:08 left. It was a big night for receiver Terrance Edwards, who caught seven balls for 92 yards, rendering another superior performance as he had done throughout the season. With the game firmly under control, Richt began playing as many reserves as possible to allow them to enjoy the experience.

While the offense was having its way with the Razorbacks, the Georgia defense — led by David Pollack, Will Thompson, Jonathon Sullivan, Tony Gilbert and Sean Jones — never allowed Arkansas to mount a serious threat. Gilbert had a total of 10 tackles, five of them unassisted. The Dawgs had the advantage with a big defensive line and came up with

four sacks.

When the game was over, Richt knew that his team would serve as host in the Sugar Bowl in New Orleans. The heady experience, however, would be tempered by the uneasy circumstance of having to play Florida State, his old team. He would be trying to find a way to win a game, which meant he would be defeating old friends. "Not the easiest thing to do," he said.

(Above) Pollack, a three-time All-American, and the rest of the Bulldog defense never allowed Arkansas to mount a serious threat.

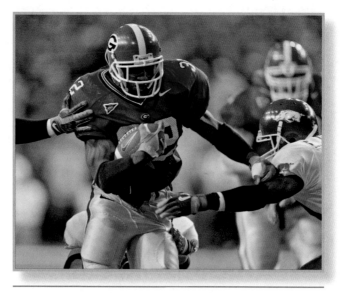

(Above) Musa Smith scored Georgia's first touchdown, and the Bulldogs never looked back.

FOOTAGE FROM
SCAN TO WATCH THE SUGAR BOWL

DOGS FINISH THE DRILL IN NEW ORLEANS

Jan. 1, 2003
Georgia 26, Florida State 13

(Left) Coach Mark Richt celebrates with the Sugar Bowl trophy after defeating Florida State, where he had previously been the offensive coordinator for Bobby Bowden.

Playing in the Sugar Bowl means that, in most cases, you are playing as the champion of the Southeastern Conference. On New Year's Day 2003, Georgia was designated the home team, as the SEC champion, against Florida State.

The Seminoles were still a dominant power in college football, and Bobby Bowden was the winningest coach in the NCAA. Bowden was still a youthful and energized head coach who could recruit and was winning at a 10-game-a-year clip or better.

Richt had been Bowden's offensive coordinator, and obviously knew a lot about the Seminole program. Some of the players he had coached when he left Tallahassee to become the Bulldogs' head coach in late 2000 were still around. Richt felt uncomfortable, emotionally, going up against his old team, but he was focused on winning the game. Victory would be a plus in furthering the establishment of his program.

Privately, he believed that his defense was better than Florida State's, and he felt that his quarterback situation was a positive. While it was not a platoon circumstance, Richt managed the game plan to include both quarterbacks — David Greene, the starter, and D.J. Shockley, the backup.

The positive reviews of this game began with the Bulldog defense. It forced three turnovers, and one of the key plays came when Bruce Thornton intercepted a FSU pass and returned it 71 yards for a touchdown. Right on the heels of that scoring break, Shockley completed a 37-yard scoring pass to Terrence Edwards. The Bulldogs led 17-7 at the half.

FSU would score a touchdown at the end of the third quarter, but Chris Clemons stopped a two-point conversion run — a key play at a propitious moment. Billy Bennett would add a pair of field goals as Georgia defeated the Seminoles 26-13.

There was obvious pride in the victory for Richt, who said it was a good feeling to defeat his former team because of the "....great respect I have for the Florida State program."

The slogan for the Georgia team had become, "Finish the Drill." The Bulldogs felt they had accomplished their mission of winning that first title under their new head coach.

It was obvious Bowden was proud of Richt, saying, "He is such a nice guy and I worried about his toughness. He proved to me this year that he can be tough when it really matters. He'll have a fine record at Georgia."

(Above and below) Musa Smith had a career game against Florida State, rushing for 145 yards. He was named the game's MVP.

117

SENIORS GO OUT AS WINNERS

Oct. 30, 2004 · Georgia 31, Florida 24

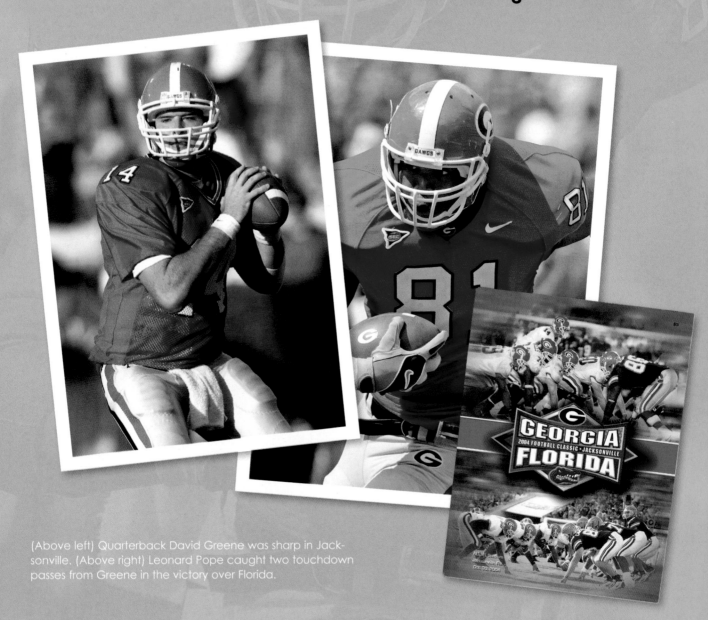

GEORGIA
FLORIDA
2004 FOOTBALL CLASSIC · JACKSONVILLE

(Above left) Quarterback David Greene was sharp in Jacksonville. (Above right) Leonard Pope caught two touchdown passes from Greene in the victory over Florida.

The Bulldogs had made back-to-back trips to the Georgia Dome in 2002 and 2003 for the SEC Championship Game. The second trip was not as much fun as the first one, as Georgia lost 34-14 to LSU in the '03 title contest.

In 2004, David Greene and Davey Pollack — along with Thomas Davis, Reggie Brown and a number of other capable players with visions of a championship on their mind — began the season with sharp focus. They were expecting big things.

LSU, which defeated the Bulldogs twice in the 2003 — in Baton Rouge 17-10 in the regular season, and in the rematch at the Georgia Dome in the SEC title game — came to Athens in early October. The Bulldogs were ready.

Greene was in top form against LSU, completing 10 of 19 passes for 172 yards and five touchdowns, a school record. The next week, the Bulldogs were a little off, playing Tennessee between the hedges. Tennessee had the emotional advantage and won 19-14. Georgia made a number of critical mistakes but was in position to score at the end of the game when Greene's last pass attempt for the winning touchdown was batted away.

(Above) Reggie Brown and his teammates were expecting big things in 2004.

The Bulldogs went to Jacksonville in October, remembering they had endured a seven-year win streak by Florida. Bulldog seniors were keen on going out a winner. It wasn't easy, but Greene was sharp and tight end Leonard Pope had a two-touchdown afternoon, running a flag route, known as 43 Betsy.

Florida rallied in the second half, scoring 17 points to Georgia's 10. With 8:37 remaining in the fourth quarter, Greene hit Fred Gibson on a 15-yard scoring pass that put the Dawgs up 31-21. Gibson's fingertip catch in the end zone was a thing of beauty.

It was the last time that players like Greene and Pollack played in Jacksonville, and they were determined to end the Gators' winning streak. The game might have been different had the Bulldogs scored a touchdown near the end of the first half. Leading 21-7, Greene marched the Bulldogs down to the 1-yard line, but fumbled the snap and Florida recovered.

All is well that ends well, however, and the Bulldogs celebrated a much deserved victory with good fortune to follow, as Georgia was invited to Tampa where they would play in the Outback Bowl — a fitting exit for Greene and Pollack, the "Beloved Dawgs," and their friends.

(Above) Fred Gibson chats with an official after his 15-yard fingertip touchdown catch.

SHOCKLEY SHOCKS LSU IN TITLE GAME

Dec. 5, 2005 · Georgia 34, LSU 14

(Left) The 2005 SEC Champion Georgia Bulldogs. (Below) Quarterback D.J. Shockley was named the game's MVP.

Georgia's third trip to the Georgia Dome was one to remember, as the Bulldogs defeated the LSU Tigers in a 34-14 upset. But the Dogs had to manage several challenges just to get to the SEC Championship Game.

Quarterback D.J. Shockley, who had to overcome injuries often in his career, had missed the game against Florida with a knee injury — which significantly influenced the outcome of the game — as the Gators won 14-10.

The Bulldogs then lost a 31-30 heartbreaker the next Saturday in Athens, when Auburn kicked a 20-yard field goal — after converting on a fourth-and-10 situation — with six seconds left on the clock.

Even with the loses to Florida and Auburn, the Bulldogs made it to the SEC Championship Game to face favored LSU, which had won the SEC West with a 7-1 record and were led by quarterback Jamarcus Russell, a remarkable college football talent.

Shockley played perhaps his best game, completing 6 of 12 passes for 112 yards and two touchdowns, and ran for another score. Brandon Coutu kicked two field goals, and Tim Jennings intercepted an LSU pass and returned it 15 yards for a touchdown.

Georgia took charge of the game early, with Shockley throwing two touchdown passes to wide receiver Sean Bailey for an early 14-0 lead. Shockley's 7-yard scoring run gave the Dawgs a 21-7 lead by halftime.

In the second half, the Bulldogs continued to outplay the Tigers, scoring 10 more points while LSU could only produce one additional touchdown. The 34-14 final was one of the most convincing wins Georgia has had in postseason play.

If there was anybody happier than Shockley, it was coach Mark Richt, whose winning pleasure was enhanced by his affection for his quarterback.

"He had gone through a lot with injuries and is such a deserving player — I just had warm feelings out on the field, seeing him being congratulated," Richt said. "He is a deserving young man, and I am very happy for him."

When D.J. was competing for the starting job with David Greene, there were many of "Shock's" friends who advised him to transfer and play at another school, but Shockley had always wanted to be a Bulldog and had no serious interest in leaving the Georgia campus.

In addition to leading his team to a championship, D.J. received his degree and has always been eager to trumpet his emotions and feelings for Georgia. "I love the University of Georgia and I'll always be a Bulldog," he told a sold-out banquet in his honor in the spring, following the end of his collegiate playing career.

(Above) Shockley threw for two touchdown passes and ran for another score against LSU. (Below) Shockley gleefully embraces coach Mark Richt during the postgame celebration.

BOWLING OVER THE HOKIES

Dec. 30, 2006 · Georgia 31, Virginia Tech 24

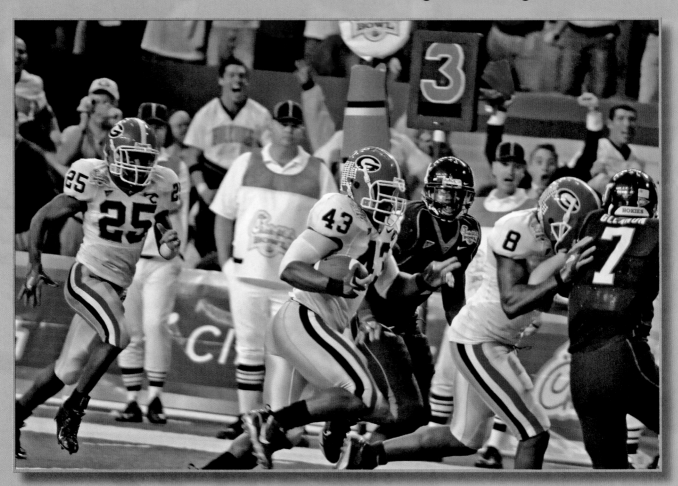

(Above) Tony Taylor returns one of his two interceptions against Virginia Tech.

In December 2006, Mark Richt announced he was naming Mike Bobo as Georgia's offensive coordinator. Bobo had worked as quarterback coach under Richt since he had left Florida State to become the Bulldog head coach in late 2000.

In 2006, the Bulldogs experienced an up-and-down season, finishing 8-4 before receiving a Chick-fil-A Bowl invitation to play Virginia Tech, a team that has always been respected for its defensive expertise. The Hokies are annually among the top teams in the Atlantic Coast Conference when it comes to competing for the league championship.

"They are like SEC teams," Bobo said one day while watching videotape of Georgia's upcoming bowl opponent. "They are fast and quick. They really get off the ball."

As the scouting session wore on, a cogent Bobo said, "We have got to come up with something to neutralize that great rush that they have."

In the first half, Georgia's offense turned laggard while the defense was yielding. The Hokies scored three touchdowns — lighting quick on five plays, eight plays and one play — for a 21-3 lead at intermission. It looked like a long night for the Bulldogs, but the locker room was upbeat at the half as players admitted to "shooting themselves in the foot."

The Bulldogs would score 28 points in the second half while the defense held the Hokies to a single field goal for a 31-24 victory.

The Georgia comeback got kick-started in the third quarter when Brandon Coutu made a 51-yard field goal with 6:10 left on the clock. One of the things that was discussed at the half was an onside-kick opportunity. Be alert, the coaches had advised. After conferring with his assistants with Virginia Tech leading 21-6, Richt felt it was a favorable risk and flashed the signal to Brian Mimbs, whose onside surprise effort was recovered at the Georgia 48. Quarterback Matthew Stafford then directed a six-play drive and the lead was suddenly 21-13, and the Dawgs had gained the momentum.

A Tony Taylor interception in the fourth quarter enabled the Bulldogs to gain favorable field position at the Virginia Tech 43. A Stafford pass completion of 41 yards to Martrez Milner had the Dawgs at the Virginia Tech 3-yard line. Then came that alacritous Hokie rush, but Bobo anticipated the charge and had Stafford hand off to Kregg Lumpkin on a delay. Lumpkin walked into the end zone untouched. Coach Bobo had neutralized the Hokie rush! After a successful two-point pass from Stafford to Milner, the score was now tied 21-21.

On Tech's next possession, Charles Johnson sacked the Hokie quarterback and Quentin Moses recovered the fumble at the Virginia Tech 19-yard line. Five plays later, Coutu kicked a field goal to give the Dawgs a 24-21 lead.

Before you could say "Hail to Georgia Down in Dixie," Tony Taylor had another interception and returned it to the Hokie 1-yard-line. Brannon Southerland scored the touchdown to make it Georgia 31, Virginia Tech 21. Tech later added a field goal, but after the Bulldog defense, led by Taylor, had gained the upper hand.

It turned out to be one of the greatest comebacks in Bulldog bowl history.

(Above) Brannon Southerland on the run against the Hokies. Southerland's fourth-quarter touchdown gave the Bulldogs a 31-21 lead.

HENDERSON'S

SCAN TO WATCH

WINNING CATCH

A SPECIAL WIN OVER SABAN

Sept. 22, 2007 · Georgia 26, Alabama 23

(Above) The scoreboard and the smile on Mikey Henderson's face says it all after he caught the game-winning touchdown against Alabama in 2007.

As Mark Richt began his 12th season as head coach of the Georgia Bulldogs and reflected back on his career, he had many Saturday successes to identify as milestone victories. Some of those would relate to games that won championships or led to championships. Others would be "emotional" highlights.

Reflecting back, one of his emotional highlights would be his second trip to Tuscaloosa in 2007. Georgia's 26-23 defeat of Alabama included all the trimmings — an overtime victory with a 25-yard touchdown pass from Matthew Stafford to Mikey Henderson.

If Richt were to reveal his inner thoughts, you would expect him, as it is with many coaches, to confirm that beating Nick Saban is something special. When you beat Saban, you are beating the best. I can remember Richt's unending smile after the 2004 LSU game between the hedges when the Bulldogs slammed Saban's LSU Tigers 45-16 — a well-coached team gets taken to the woodshed by team that rendered a superior performance.

In the 2007 Alabama game, Saban was getting his program established at Tuscaloosa, but the Bulldogs were also a young team with a mature quarterback in Stafford, who was complemented by capable playmakers like Knowshon Moreno.

At Tuscaloosa, Georgia scored first on a touchdown pass from Stafford to Thomas Brown in the first quarter, which was followed by a Brandon Coutu field goal and a 10-3 halftime lead. The Bulldogs would add another 10 points in the second half on another field goal, 47 yards, by Coutu and a 6-yard run by Moreno.

Alabama fought back with 10 points in the fourth quarter and the game went into overtime when Coutu missed a 47-yard field-goal attempt as time expired in regulation.

The Tide scored first in overtime on a 42-yard field goal. Georgia went for the juggler right away. On first down, Stafford hit Mikey Henderson on a 25-yard scoring toss. The play was "Yo to L, 142 Takeoff." Georgia had run the play earlier in the game without significant result. It was a play-action call to the weakside. Assistant coach Mike Bobo guessed that Alabama would likely press hard in this situation. He guessed right. When Stafford faked to the running back off right tackle, the strong safety overreacted to the inside to provide run support, just enough to allow for a one-on-one matchup with Henderson and the corner. Henderson gained a step on his man and Stafford threw a perfect pass. Henderson made a fine catch, and the Georgia celebration ensued, as the sideline poured onto the field and the players engulfed the ebullient Henderson with uncontrolled jubilation.

(Above) Head coach Mark Richt enjoyed an "emotional highlight" by beating Alabama and Nick Saban in 2007.

A Total Team Effort

Nov. 12, 2011 · Georgia 45, Auburn 7

(Above) Quarterback Aaron Murray was red hot against Auburn, completing 14 of 18 passes for 224 yards and four touchdowns, including one to Michael Bennett (right) for 27 yards.

The Georgia-Auburn game in 2011 was, perhaps, the best game of the season for the Bulldogs. All players got high marks for their performances. While no game is ever perfect or played flawlessly, the Auburn game, at least from the Georgia perspective, was as near perfect as any game in recent memory.

It all began with quarterback Aaron Murray, who had his best day by completing 14 of 18 passes for 224 yards and four touchdowns: Tavarres King for 8 yards, Michael Bennett for 27 yards, Bruce Figgins for 15 yards and Malcolm Mitchell for 25 yards.

With crisp and overpowering blocking up front, the Bulldogs rushed for 304 yards on 56 attempts, and 528 yards of total offense.

"Man, that was fun," said coach Mark Richt after the game.

The Bulldogs, after starting the season 0-2, had rallied to win eight straight, putting them in position to earn a berth in the SEC Championship Game with a victory over Kentucky the next week. The Auburn win gave the Dawgs momentum. You could see it in the players' eyes in the locker room as they celebrated victory. "Men, all we have to do is take care of business," Murray said after the game, referring to the forthcoming Kentucky game. The Dawgs had begun to smell the SEC East title.

Georgia scored first against the Tigers with the Murray-to-King touchdown pass midway through the first quarter. Auburn answered that scoring drive with one of its own, with 6:13 remaining in the opening period.

You could have gotten a slap-in-the-face reaction if you had suggested, at that time, that Auburn was done for the day, that the Tigers would not cross the Georgia goal line again. After all, Auburn arrived in Sanford Stadium with five wins and was ranked No. 24 in the country. Lest anyone be reminded, the Georgia-Auburn game, more often than not, has produced some classic struggles. Historically, there have been an abundance of games settled by a touchdown or a field goal, or less.

But when it was over, the Georgia margin of victory was 38 points. You have to go back to 1946 to find a game in which there was a greater margin of victory, when the Bulldogs were victorious in Columbus 41-0.

The Bulldogs' dominance in 2011 came about with the home team making its fewest mistakes in a game in years. The "team effort" cliche was happily invoked in the locker room following the game, the cheering led by Richt, who complimented the defense for refusing to yield, and toasting the offense for putting points on the scoreboard and controlling the line of scrimmage.

(Above) Bruce Figgins on his 15-yard touchdown reception.

About The Author

Loran Smith, a longtime member of the University of Georgia Athletic Association staff, is also a broadcaster, columnist and freelance writer. He spends time at the major golf tournaments, Major League Baseball spring training camps and a number of other popular sporting events and venues, but all are subordinated to his love and interest in the Georgia Bulldogs.

He has worked in a variety of jobs with the Bulldogs, from business manager to serving as executive secretary of the Georgia Bulldog Clubs. He was elected to the State of Georgia Sports Hall of Fame in 1997 and has authored or co-authored a dozen books, most of them about the Georgia Bulldogs, including Whitman Publishing's *University of Georgia Football Vault* and the *Florida-Georgia Rivalry Football Vault*.

He and his wife, Myrna, live a mile from the campus where they met as students. Daughter Camille and son Kent are UGA graduates. The Smiths have four grandchildren: Alex, Zoe, Sophie and Penny.

Acknowledgments

No chronicling of any subject can legitimately take place without invoking appreciation for those who blazed the trail of history. In the case of the written word about Georgia athletics, one cannot adequately cover the subject without paying tribute to the Bulldogs' two noted historians, the late Dr. John Stegeman and Dan Magill.

Stegeman camped out at the university library for days, weeks and months, which led to years, bringing forth gems of research that became invaluable. Magill never threw anything away and developed exhaustive files for latter-day writers to glean the important facts and lore of the exploits of the Bulldogs. This work, like so many others, would not be possible without the contributions of those two titans of Georgia history. We all continue to draw on their works.

Additionally, there is Claude Felton, who has been keeper of the files and expanding the content after suc-

ceeding Magill. No professional has ever been more in step with being a custodian of history, fact and lore than this native son, who grew up in Savannah.

Stories can't be told without photos, and we are indebted to the work and efforts of Steve Colquitt, Felton's longtime associate. He was patient and thorough, as is his custom. His contribution to this work allowed for the best of treasured photos from the UGA Sports Communications Office.

In addition, we pay tribute to the following in the Bulldog family: Greg McGarity, athletic director, a hometown boy making good at his alma mater; Alan Thomas, associate athletic director of External Operations; Sports Communications Office manager Karen Huff, along with Ben Beaty and Kate Burkholder, capable members of Claude Felton's staff; Mark Maxwell, the keeper of the storehouse of the Bulldogs' film and video archives; Tim Pennell and Chantel Dunham of the University's Research Library; and Bill Simpson, former editor of *Georgia Alumni Record*.

And, to my family: my wife Myrna, who managed the manuscript through the computer, and my daughter Camille Martin for editing assistance and fact checking.

Photo & Video Credits

All photographs in this book provided with permission by the University of Georgia Sports Communications Office, except for the image of Verron Haynes on page 110, which was taken by Radi Nabulsi, and the photo of Mikey Henderson on page 124, which was submitted by Dean Legge (dawgpost.com).

Whitman Publishing would like to thank Claude Felton and Steve Colquitt from the UGA Sports Communications Office for their extra effort to provide us with the photographs to illustrate this book, and special thanks to Mark Maxwell from Maxwell Sound Recording Studio (firsttune.com) in Athens, Georgia, for creating the videos.

The Georgia Athletic Association wishes to thank the following for photo assistance: Perry McIntyre, Getty Images, Steve Davis, Dan Evans, Steve Guyer, Jim Hipple, Phillip Faulkner, John Kelley, Radi Nabulsi, Evey Wilson, Kevin Works and Dale Zanine.